YOU AND YOUR LEGAL RIGHTS

Peter Wade

WARWICKSHIRE LIBRARY & INFO SERVICE	
Bertrams	06.11.05
340	£9.99

Emerald Publishing
Brighton BN2 4EG

© Peter Wade 2005 First Edition

All rights reserved. No part of this publication may be reproduced in a retrieval system or transmitted by any means, electronic or mechanical, photocopying or other wise, without the prior permission of the copyright holder.

British Cataloguing in Publication data. A catalogue record is available for this book from the British Library.

ISBN 1903909 61 9

Printed in the United kingdom by CATS Ltd, Swindon, Wilts

Cover Design by Bookworks

Whilst every effort has been made to ensure that the information in this book is accurate at the time of going to print, the author and publisher recognise that the information can become out of date. The book is therefore sold on the understanding that no responsibility for errors and omissions is assumed and no responsibility is held for the information held within.

CONTENTS

1	You and the Courts – The English Legal System	1
2	You and Your Home – Land Law	11
3	You and the Police – Criminal Law	33
4	You and Your Neighbours – Civil Law – The Law of Tort	51
5	You and Your Neighbours – The Neighbour Principle	63
6	You and Your Job – Employment Law	71
7	You and Your Family – Matrimonial Law	81
8	You and Your Leisure – Consumer Law	91
9	You and Your Litigation – Small Claims Court	97
10	You and Your Death – Wills, Probate and Intestacy	107
11	You and Your Car – Motoring	119
12	You and Your Business	127
	Appendix	137
	Glossary	141
	Index	153

1

YOU AND THE COURTS
English Legal System

The Courts and the Judges.
The Highest Court in the Land is the House of Lords but most of us will be dealing with the bottom of the pile so I have outlined the courts in that way.

Tribunals.
These include employment tribunals, which deal with disputes between employers and employees covering unfair dismissal and discrimination. They are intended to be simple and easy to use and also cover such areas as immigration, rent, land assessment, social security and mental health.

Employment Appeals Tribunal.
These hear Appeals from Employment Tribunals and comprise a High Court Judge and two lay members with knowledge of industrial relations.

Magistrates Courts.
These are the lowest Courts in the criminal justice system and they also have civil jurisdiction in family matters dealing with maintenance and adoption and they are also responsible for licensing matters such as granting liquor licences for restaurants, betting shops, casinos. Their licensing functions are being taken over by Local Authorities.

Crown Courts
This is the more senior Criminal Court that deals with criminal cases heard by a Judge and Jury and it also acts as an Appeal from the Magistrates Court.

County Courts

These are part of the civil system and are all over England and Wales. They are presided over by a circuit judge who has the power to hear all but the most important sort of cases.

Fast track cases are allocated to the County Courts such as money claims between £5,000 and £15,000 and also re-possession cases. Most Landlord and Tenant disputes, disputes over Wills, bankruptcy and winding up of companies. They have the power to grant divorces and make orders concerning property and children. In more complex cases it may be transferred to the High Court.

Court of Protection.

A Receiver can be granted for relatives where a person is incapable of taking care of his or her own property. It is also the place where Enduring Powers of Attorney are registered.

Coroners Courts

This is where inquests are held if deaths occur not due to natural causes. It is not strictly speaking a Trial. It is investigative procedure

High Court.

This sits at the Royal Courts of Justice in London and at other centres throughout England and Wales. It is divided into three sections: Queens Bench, Chancery and Family. Multi-track cases are allocated to the High Court.

Queens Bench Division

This is the biggest of the three divisions and covers general civil claims for damages in tort and contract. Within the Queens Bench Division there are specialist courts:

- The Commercial Court dealing with commercial matters.
- The Admiralty Court, which deals with shipping, disputes.
- The Divisional Court, which deals with judicial, reviews and appeals from the Magistrates on points of law

Chancery Division

This deals with such matters as tax, land mortgages, property trusts and Wills. There are specialist courts within the Chancery Division

- The Companies Court deals with winding up director's disqualification's and administration etc.
- The Patents Court which deals with disputes concerning copyright, passing off etc.

Family Division
This deals with all family matters particularly disputes in divorce proceedings. It also covers Wards of Court and deals with adoption orders.

JUDICIAL REVIEWS
A process for reviewing administrative decisions and can be used to challenge decisions of government departments.

Court of Appeal.
This hears appeals from the County Court, High Court and Crown Court. Most generally involve an important point of legal principle. It is divided into the criminal and civil divisions and is situated in the Royal Courts of Justice in London. Three judges known as Lords Justices generally hear an appeal.

House of Lords
The Lords of Appeal in Ordinary (Law Lords) are the legal members of the House of Lords and form the highest court in England. The House of Lords hears not only English appeals but also Scottish civil but not criminal appeals. It is generally only hears appeal on points of law of general public importance. Permission must be obtained to pursue such an appeal.

Privy Council
The Judicial Committee of the Privy Council hears appeals from what remains of the Colonies.

The Court of Justice of the European Union
This sits in Luxembourg. It covers matters of European Law such as interpretation of the law and their decisions are final and take precedence even over the House of Lords decisions.

LEGAL PROFESSION
The Lord Chancellor:
The Lord High Chancellor of Great Britain is appointed by the Queen on the advice of the Prime Minister He combines the legislative, executive and Judiciary, and presides over the House of Lords. He is a Member of the Cabinet, and also Chief Legal Officer, Head of the Judiciary, Member of the Judiciary Committee of the Privy Council, Head of the Chancery Division of the High Court, and Member of the Court of Appeal. He never actually sits as a Judge other than in the House of Lords and in the Judicial Committee of the Privy Council.

Judges:
- *Lord Chief Justice.*
  Head of the Court of Appeal.
  Court of Appeal Queens Bench Division.
  Member of the House of Lords.
- *Master of the Rolls.*
  Head of the Court of Appeal and also supervises the admission of solicitors to the Rolls of the Supreme Court.
- *President of the Family Division*
- *Lords of Appeal in ordinary known as Law Lords:*
  Life Peers adjudicate in appeal cases heard in the House of Lords. Members of the Judiciary Committee of Privy Council. There are 9 of them.
- *Lord Justices of Appeal.*
  Judges in the Appeal Courts 23
  Judges in the High Court (known as Puisne Judges):
     In the Chancery Division................................. 12
     In the Queens Bench Division............................ 45
     Family Division 16
  Hold office during good behaviour and retire at the age of 75.
  Circuit Judges. Retire at 72 – Extension to 75

Recorders:
Under the Crown Courts Act 1971 – these are designated part-time judges at the Crown Court

Attorney General – Solicitor General:
These are the Law Officers and political appointments

- *Attorney General:*
Is the chief legal advisor to the Government and is responsible for the Crown Prosecution Service. Is a member of the House of Commons, represents the Crown in Civil matters, and advises the Cabinet. Certain criminal offences must be reported to the Attorney General and his consent is required.

Deputy Attorney General:
- *Masters of the Supreme Court.*
They adjudicate on all matters preliminary to a Trial
- *Chancery Division Masters.*
- *Taxing Masters.*
They check costs paid by parties to a trial

Director of Public Prosecutions.
He is the official responsible for the Crown Prosecution Service. He is responsible for all criminal proceedings on behalf of the Police.

THE LEGAL PROFESSION:
Two Branches of the Legal Profession:
Barristers & Solicitors:
Solicitors
Descended from Attorneys, Solicitors and Proctors. Usually completed a Law Degree or if a non law graduate, completed the common professional examination, undertaken one year legal practice course, followed by two terms as a trainee solicitor.

Duties of a solicitor:
Most are employed in private practice. Solicitors have rights of audience in the Magistrates Court, County Courts. Limited rights of audience in the Crown Court and the Supreme Court.

Barristers:
They join one of the four Inns of Court:

Grays Inn
Lincoln's Inn
Inner Temple
Middle Temple.

Barristers
Have to keep terms in their Inn and to qualify for call to the Bar must be as a Law graduate – non law graduate – completed the common professional examination, followed by a years professional training course before undertaking one years pupillage in Chambers. After six months, Barristers have the right of audience in any Court of Law in England and Wales. They may take instructions only from a solicitor not from a lay client direct.

Duties of a Barrister:
Barrister is essentially an advocate whose task is to represent his/her client's case effectively in Court. Their work includes drafting of opinions on difficult points of law. The settling of pleadings and the advice and evidence on procedural matters.

The differences are:
- Barristers are advocates
- Barristers have rights of audience in all Courts
- Barristers specialise in certain branches of the Law
- Barristers deal with legal matters only
- Barristers are instructed by solicitors
- Barristers cannot sue for their fees, solicitors can
- Barristers may not be liable for negligence under the case
- Barristers are controlled by the Inns of Court

Queens Counsel:
Barristers have acquired a certain substantial practice – application may be made to the Lord Chancellor to take silk i.e. become Queens Counsel. They will have the assistance of junior counsel who will be briefed with them. They are called with Q.C. Leader or Silk.

Licensed Conveyancers:
Authorised to carry out legal formalities relating to the transfer of land.
De-regulation of Legal Services in Court and Legal Services Act 1990 has removed many restrictions on the rights for audiences on certain County Court proceedings

Legal Service Ombudsman:
The Court and Legal Service Act 1990 also provides for the Lord Chancellor to appoint a Legal Service Ombudsman to investigate allegations into a matter in which any professional legal body has dealt with any complaint made against any of its members.

The Legal system
Seeking Advice
The community Legal Service:
From April 2000 the Community Legal service made access to legal advice available to the public through the creation of local networks of legal services. The Legal service commission replaced the Legal aid Board.

Advice Agencies
Law Centres
Law centres offer legal advice and all have contracts with the CLS after having been audited for quality assurance. Therer are about 52 law centres in England and Wales found in inner city area in the main and generally funded by local authorities, They are run by lawyers and advice workers who specialise in social welfare law for example housing and immigrant.

Legal Advice centres
Volunteer lawyers who offer free advice and assistance. They help with form filling and will write letters. Usually run by church groups charities etc.

Citizens Advice Bureaux
If the problem is more complex you may be referred elsewhere. Their website is www.nacab.org.uk.
You can obtain advice on www.adviceguide.org.uk.

The Legal Internet
This can help you formulate the nature of your problem. You can initiate a claim in the small claims court or start possession proceedings against your tenant. The Lord Chancellors department website allows you to fill informs on line at www.open.gov.uk.lcd/lcdseafr.htm and allows you to submit it for processing.

Alternative Dispute Resolution (ADR)
ADR can take many forms.

In-court arbitration – the small claims procedure
This is used when a money claim does not exceed £5,000 and where a personal injury claim or a housing disrepair claim is under £1,000

Out of Court arbitration.
This can be used when the parties to a contract settle by arbitration. Landlord and tenant may agree that an arbitrator should fix a new rent. The arbitrator's decision is final and binding on the parties although the process takes place out of court.
Other forms of arbitration may be more informal i.e. a complaints procedure. Ombudsman services are another form of arbitration.

Mediation
This was to be a central part of the civil Procedure Rules (CPR) but the uptake has not been great as it is relatively new and it still viewed with a degree of suspicion.
Mediation in divorce is being widely encouraged as a way to settle disputes over the matrimonial home or questions concerning the welfare and future wellbeing of the children.

ACAS
He advisory Conciliation and Arbitration service (ACAS) was set up to act as mediator I industrial disputes. Every application to an employment tribunal is first sent to ACAS to determine whether there is any possibility of a negotiated settlement.

Commissions to assist in discrimination cases
Equal Opportunities Commission
Commission for Racial Equality
Disability Rights commission

Specialist Groups and organisations
Certain organisations help their own members and other such as Victim support offer advice to the public. The RAC or AA for instance may offer legal advice to members

Trade Unions
Free Representation Unit
It is set up by the bar and deals with cases referred to them by other advice agencies such as a law centre or the CAB. It does not accept cases direct from the public.

Free Property advice
The Royal Institution of Chartered Surveyors runs a voluntary advice service on property matters for those unable to obtain professional assistance in the normal way. Again usually referred by the CAB.

CAFCASS
The Children and Family Court Advisory and support services for England and Wales. It focuses on representing the needs, wishes and feelings of children in family proceedings.

Dealing with the legal profession
In England and Wales there are basically two types of lawyers, solicitors and barristers.

Solicitors
Solicitors do contentious and non-contentious work. Most of the work never involves the courts that is most solicitors work is no contentious. This involves such tasks as drawing up wills, conveyancing, Contentious work involves litigation that is going to court and can be criminal or matrimonial or other civil work for instance a claim for personal injury or a boundary dispute.

Solicitors do all the preparation work and brief barrister to appear in the courts.

Most solicitors are in partnerships and or may be sole practitioners.

Solicitors now have the right to appear in the higher courts 1,600 in a profession of 80,000 have been given the status to appear in the higher courts, mainly in the criminal courts. Solicitors are obliged to inform clients of the charging procedure and their complaints handling procedure.

Barristers
They are advocate lawyers who appear in the higher courts. Barristers are known as counsel and they do both advocacy and give opinions.

YOU AND YOUR LEGAL RIGHTS

Funding legal proceedings
Publicly funded legal services (formerly legal aid)
   The former legal aid scheme has been replaced by two new schemes to secure the provisions of publicity funded legal services for people who qualify. They are:

- a community legal service fund for civil and family cases and
- a criminal defence scheme for people suspected or accused of crime.

Excluded are personal injury claims, cases arising out of running a business or partnership, boundary disputes and actions for libel and slander.

There are two hurdles:
- Meeting the financial test
- Fulfilling the merit test. That is your chances of success in pursuing your claim

The statutory charge
Even if you win your case you may have a charge put on your property that you have to repay. In matrimonial matters if the amount you receive is over £000 you will have to repay the difference.

Conditional fee agreements
Lawyers charge an uplift on their fees if you win your case. The loser still pays the winning sides cost but
   Initially it was 20 % uplift now 5% but in cases where there was a minimal risk of losing so the present situation is in a state of uncertainty.

Costs in court
The legal expenses payable for the services of a solicitor and barrister in court are known as costs. In a court action the losing party usually has to pay the costs of the successful party. In legal parlance the costs follow the event. Current reforms are therer to prevent the unnecessary running up of excessive litigation costs.
   The courts now have greater freedom to award costs and may penalise parties who, didn't not follow the correct procedures, exaggerated the value of the claim, been uncooperative, not tried to settle the claim where appropriate pursued a particular allegation unreasonably.

2

BUYING & SELLING YOUR HOME

The law regards transactions which involve the buying and selling of properties, that is land, differently from other transactions such as the buying and selling of goods. There are certain formalities and the process is known as conveying property or conveyancing.

This is an area of law that is constantly being looked at as it affects every one of us who buy and sell homes. The two ways that we normally hold land are as Freeholders or Leaseholders. There is now a third way of owning and managing property, which is Commonhold. The Commonhold and Leasehold Reform Act of 2002 intends to give the benefit to Leaseholders enjoyed by Freeholders.

Another significant statute is the Land Registration Act 2002. It is hoped that electronic conveyancing will streamline and speed up the process of home transfers. The theory is that in a decade, Contracts, Transfers, Leases and Mortgages could be replaced by "virtual" documents by lawyers having direct access to Land Registry.

It is claimed that new technology is already being used to improve conveyancing practice. The online National Land Information Service (NLIS) draws together information about land from a variety of sources to provide "one stop shop" for anyone carrying out Searches and enquiries. It is now possible to access Land Registry records from the Land Registry direct which provides details of 18 million Registered Titles and allows you to order Official Copies and to carry out electronic Searching

Registered or Unregistered Land.

Not all land in England and Wales is yet registered, although three quarters of property is. The Land Registry Index Map indicates which properties are registered and which are not. It is necessary to inspect this Index Map to establish whether or not a particular property is registered and to obtain the Title Number of the property.

Registered Land.
The Register is in four parts. The Property Register, The Proprietorship Register, The Charges Register and the File Plan. This comprises the Title Deeds of the property.

Unregistered land
This is obviously is a bundle of Deeds that form a record of the previous sales, mortgages and other dealings.

Freehold or Leasehold
Most properties are Freehold this gives you an absolute Title to the property, that is you own both the house and the ground it stands on. If it is Leasehold then there is a Landlord above you who owns the Freehold. Flats are usually on a long Lease.

Although you own the Freehold of the property, there may be "rights" over the property, such as a Charge, that is a mortgage or security, rights of way by neighbours, matrimonial matters, such as your wife and children living at the property.

Rights & Liabilities.
In theory you can do what you wish with the property but subject to other legislation, such as Planning, Environment Acts, Restrictive Covenants, rights of way, Charges, Building Regulations Consents.

Commonhold
The Government enacted measures in 2002 for a new form of land holding to be known as 'Commonhold'. This is an entirely new concept of owning or managing property, although it does exist in other jurisdictions. So far I have not come across commonhold as it is a very new concept and it will be interesting to how it turns out.

Buying a Newly Built House
1. Guarantees – newly built homes come with a guarantee, which provide insurance against major damage arising from structural defects. The normal guarantee period is ten years.
2. Better access to new homes – the Disability Act 1986. Guidance has been issued to help house builders to promote new building regulations to improve access to new homes.

Stamp Duty Land Tax
Previously merely called Stamp Duty. Stamp Duty land Tax applies to land transactions after December 1st 2003. It is designed to prevent some of the avoidance opportunities of Stamp Duty.

Details can be found on www.inlandrevenue.gov.uk/so.

Buyer's solicitors have to complete a detailed revenue form within 30 days of purchase, even if there is no duty. The SDLT rates are:

1%, 3% or 4% of the price, if this exceeds £120,000, £250,000 or £500,000 respectively.

Home Information Packs
Known as HIPS.

These are intended to speed up the conveyancing process.

The pack should contain such things as the Draft Contract, Searches and Home Condition report.

It is anticipated that the packs are likely to cost between £350 to £1000 pounds, and non-production of the pack could result in a £200 fine.

The system will come into force on the 1st January 2007.

E-Conveyancing
The target date for E-Conveyancing is 2007, and the theory is that it should be quicker and cheaper, but it may be open to fraud, because of the digital signature.

Employing professional services – Estate Agents
These are also affected by the section on goods and services, the buyer does not strictly employ the Estate Agent but there are legal implications.

Particulars of Property
The law has become stricter in making demands on Estate Agents to curb extravagance in their language. Under the Property Mis-Descriptions Act 1991 an Estate Agent is liable to be prosecuted if he or she mis-describes a property that is makes a misleading statement in the course of Estate Agency business. An Estate Agent has a duty of care to the seller in discharging his duties. An Estate Agent usually put disclaimers in his particulars to cover himself.

Complaining about Estate Agents
Some of them belong to the Ombudsman for Estate Agents Scheme. The Office of Fair Trading has the power to ban an Estate Agent.

Surveyors
Different types of valuations/survey

- Mortgage Valuation Report – you may not get to see a copy of this report but it is accepted law that the surveyors, even though instructed by the Building Society have a duty of care to the buyer to carry out the inspection with reasonable skill and care and not to overlook any obvious defects
- House Buyers Report and Valuation – this is a more thorough report than a mere valuation
- Structural Survey
- Environmental Survey

Conveyancers
Solicitors and Licensed Conveyancers are involved in various stages of the house buying process. They generally act for:

- The seller
- The mortgage lender
- The buyer

It is fairly common that the same solicitor act for the lender, that is the Mortgage Company, and the buyer, there may be a conflict.

The theory is that at the time of a conveyancing transaction will be cut substantially The Land Registration Act 2002 is intended to help curb gazumping.

The Conveyancers' task is carrying out searches, preliminary enquiries. These involve:

- Checking on the title of the seller
- Obtaining a Local Land Charge Search
- Obtaining answers from the seller on the Property Information Form

Drawing up a Binding Contract
A Contract in a sale of Land to be binding

- Must be in writing
- The written document must contain all the particulars
- Must be signed by both parties
- Identical documents must be signed by each party

Exchange of Contracts
Once each party signs and Contracts are exchanged the Contract becomes irrevocable. The deposit is paid and the completion date will be set in the Contract for the balance of the purchase price.

Insurance
As soon as the Contracts are exchanged you become responsible for the property and you must insure that the property is insured on from exchange of Contracts.

The seller is considered to be holding it in trust for the purchaser and must take proper care of it on behalf of the purchaser until completion.

Completion
The point at which the property changes hands. This will take place on the date specified and involves the buyer handing over the balance of the purchase price and receiving the Title Deeds. You are legally bound to complete the transaction.

Auctions
Property can be bought at auction. It is essential before hand to:

- Have the property surveyed before the auction
- Inspect the document at the office of the conveyancers to the seller
- Arrange finance

Once the hammer falls on your bid price you are committed to the purchase, this involves:

- Ten per cent of the price being paid there and then
- The balance within twenty eight days

Negligence
Negligence claims are usually dealt with under Goods and Services but the most common are solicitors being sued over 'failures in standards' and 'routine conveyancing tasks' and surveyors tend to be sued for 'failure to report defects in the property'.

When the market is in decline 'overvaluations'

Time Limits for Professional Negligence Claims
Six-year period of time within an action for Profession Negligence should be brought starts to run from the date when the Contracts are exchanged. After the six year period the claim 'statute barred' that is will not be able to proceed.

Raising the Finance
Obviously most people raise the finance by way of a mortgage

Co-Ownership
Some people buy properties together and they have to be either 'Tenants in Common' or 'Joint Tenants', which will be discussed later.

Rights and Obligations of the Lender when Borrower and Lender enter into a Mortgage Deed.
The Lender takes legal charge over the property. This provides security of the land in case the borrower defaults on the mortgage payments.
    Repossession of a mortgaged property will only be considered as a last resort.

Court Order
A lender must apply to the Court for an Order for Possession even when the borrower is clearly in default. The Court then exercises a discretion to adjourn the Grant of the Possession Order to allow the parties to reach some other financial accommodation such as paying off current instalments or selling the property.

The Pitfalls in Purchasing
The Question of who buys and who sells is obviously of course of paramount importance.

Who buys
You may buy the property in your sole name. Your choices of ownership are 'Joint Tenants' or 'Tenants in Common'.

Joint Tenants
This is usually on the basis upon which husband and wife choose to buy the matrimonial home. The property is then owned jointly, that is in equal shares. If either person dies the other share passes automatically to the survivor who then becomes the sole owner of the property.

You may sever the Joint Tenancy during your lifetime; this converts into a 'Tenancy in Common'.

Tenancy in Common
In this case each co-owner owns a separate share of the property. It does not have to be an equal share; it can reflect the value, which each party has contributed to the purchase price. Each tenant in common when they die his or her share of the property will be dealt with according to the Will, if there is one, otherwise under the rules of intestacy.

Who Sells
Usually it is the owner with the registered title who sells, but there are other parties who may have an interest in the property such as a divorced spouse.

Although of less importance these days, years ago only the husband used to have the title because of the availability of mortgages and who was working. This used to lead to a situation whereby the husband took the view that he owned the house and that the wife had no interest. The wife has an interest even though she is not on the Title Deeds. Again a whole series of cases arose whereby banks, building societies and lenders took the signature of one party, that is the person on the Title Deeds and not his spouse. This has now been resolved these days by banks and other lenders making sure that anybody else at the property takes independent legal advice and signs the appropriate forms.

Vacant Possession
It is both yours and the solicitors to make sure there is not anyone else living at the house who have a right to be there and have no intention to leave on request. Building societies etc will not lend unless there is vacant possession. What normally happens is any occupant who has a right to live in the property is also made a party to the contract.

Easements, Planning Controls and Restrictive Covenants
Land and buildings can involve other people's rights too over and under any property, and there may be existing future plans for your area such as road building schemes. All the matters will be revealed by the Local Search.

YOU AND YOUR LEGAL RIGHTS

Hedges Fences and Leylandii
New Legislation under part 8 of the Antisocial Behaviour Act 2003 has been promised and is now in force. This will enable you to take your complaint to your local authority.

The local authority will have the right to order the cutting back of the hedge, subject to £1000.00 fines for non-compliance. The suggestion is you reach agreement with your neighbour for reducing the hedge.

The office of Deputy Prime Minister has produced a leaflet 'Over the Garden Hedge' – www.odpm.gov.uk, containing advice on how to resolve the dispute amicably.

Private Rights
There may be private rights over the property. These include rights of way, mining rights, gaming rights, riparian rights (on the sides of rivers), rights to maintain and/or repair fences and hedges, rights of light.

Restrictive Covenants
These are things that you can not do on your land, such as building more than one house on the plot.

Local Authority and other designations
The Local Authority would be involved with things like compulsory purchase orders, road schemes, tree preservation orders, conservation areas, building preservation orders, drainage and listed buildings consent.

Boundaries
Just because it is registered with the Land Registry, this does not guarantee the boundaries to the property are the actual boundaries. The plan is only a general indication of the boundaries.

Selling your home
Usually you employ an estate agent who relies on a property questionairre. The general rule is that buyers are to satisfy themselves the property is in order, with no structural faults no unresolved legal issues. It is not the seller's job to tell the purchaser anything, as a rule is caveat emptor, let the buyer beware. If specifically asked you cannot give false information. Standard form of questionnaire is the Property Information Form (PIF) which has been prepared by the Law Society.

Misrepresentation
If you do not answer the questions truthfully you may be liable for misrepresentation

Fixtures and Fittings
Again you will be called upon to fill in a form detailing the fixtures and fittings which you intend to sell.

Searches and Surveys
It is for the buyers not for the sellers to make certain the results of the searches are satisfactory.

Completion and moving out
Completion is the actual day of moving when the property is sold or purchased, and vacant possession is given on that day.

Seller's Pack or Home Information Pack (HIP)
There have been proposals for a seller's pack whereby the seller will provide at his or her own expense various items to the would-be purchasers. The package would deal with such matters as surveys, searches, valuations, and details of fixtures and fittings. The theory is this will cut down the period between offering the property for sale and the sale. Pilot scheme found the packs were not popular with sellers, particularly those with cheaper properties who resented the extra cost involved. Buyers were more enthusiastic. The seller's packs were included in the Homes Bill. The theory is it will be introduced in the latest Home Bill and will become law. The main aim is to reduce the time it takes from sale agreed to exchange of contracts.

Land Registration Act 2002
This creates a system of electronic conveyancing to replace the traditional paper based system. The most significant point is that the Act introduces a new system of adverse possession for registered land on the basis that registration rather than possession should be the basis of title.

Concerns about e-conveyancing
Some concerns have been expressed about the security aspects of e-conveyancing i.e. fraud.

Landlords and their tenants

English property law is divided between freehold and leasehold. There is to be a new category of commonhold which comes under the Commonhold and Leasehold Reform Act 2002. The purpose of commonhold is to set in place a satisfactory scheme of owning and managing property to overcome the problems of the leasehold system.

Some fundamental aspects of landlord and tenant relationships

There are many kinds of lease. They cover business premises, council houses in the public sector, flats bought on long leases, private rented accommodation, agricultural estates or smallholdings.

A lease always entails at least two parties, the landlord and the tenant. The landlord grants to the tenant the exclusive use of property on certain conditions and for a certain time. There can be joint tenants, joint landlords or subtenants.

A lease is therefore bound by a time limit. This can be for a week, a month, a year, and a fixed period or as long as 999 years.

An essential aspect of a lease is the need for exclusive possession. In exchange for exclusive possession the tenant must pay a rent to the landlord. A complex network of duties binds landlord and tenant and obligations called covenants, which are found in all leases. When a lease expires, the property, which comprises the lease, must go back or revert to the landlord.

The position of a tenant is protected by legislation to a greater of lesser extent, depending on the type of lease.

Distinction between leasehold and freehold property

In freehold:

- it does not involve two parties – the property belongs to the owner
- it does not have a time limit
- rent is not payable

Distinction between lease and licence

The landlord may grant you a licence but not a lease. There have been attempts by landlords to get round the leasehold legislation by calling leases licences, but this does not matter, as the courts will look at the substance of the agreement, not what the parties call it.

Examples of licences might be a caretaker of a block of flats.

Landlord living on the premises
Generally where a landlord lives on the premises together with his tenant, the tenant occupies the property as licensee only. Example being a lodger.

Covenants
Landlords implied covenants
- Covenant for quiet enjoyment. That is the landlord should allow you uninterrupted use of the premises. It does not literally mean quiet as in no noise. A recent case against a local authority meant that the landlord would not substantially interfere with a tenant's lawful possession of the property, the noise came from other tenants, not the landlord.

Covenant not to detract from the value of the lease
Things like the landlord changing the terms of the lease without checking you, such as doing extra work, giving away your car parking spaces etc.

Fitness of premises – repairs
In short-term lettings, usually under seven years, there is an implied covenant that the premises should be fit for habitation.

Most common leasehold is a long lease of a flat, and the landlord has duties to maintain the premises but this is usually recovered from the leaseholders, by way of service charges.

Gas regulations
With regard to the installation of fitting of gas appliances, landlords are under a duty to keep and maintain all appliances and installation work in a safe condition. This relates to short-hold tenancies, that is tenancies of domestic properties.

Furniture regulations
Similarly, landlords must ensure that all furniture supplied in all let accommodation must comply with these safety regulations.

The tenant's implied covenants
- to pay the rent
- to pay certain charges – in long leases these will be service charges, in short term lettings ordinary outgoings such as gas or electricity.

Not to "commit waste"
This is a technical term meaning that the tenant should not do anything, which diminishes the value of the premises.

To allow the landlord to enter the premises
The landlord may enter the premises on reasonable notice.

Covenants concerning use
Some leases contain clauses, which forbid the tenant to use the premises in a certain way, such as business premises or for immoral purposes.

Covenants controlling assignment
Again a landlord may insist that his permission is given before it is assigned to anybody else.

Insurance
The landlord will insure but usually this is recovered from the tenant.

Terminating a tenancy
Leases usually contain clauses, which allow a landlord to regain the premises in certain circumstances. For example when the tenant fails to pay the rent uses the premises in a way which the lease does not permit. In legal terms the lease is forfeited and the landlord can re-enter, subject to the laws which protect tenants against eviction. Restrictions are coming in on the capacity of landlords to use forfeiture proceedings for non-payment of service charges.

Renting in the private sector
The government has been anxious to promote private sector lettings. It was felt that the main obstacle to developing the private rental market was the fact that landlords were reluctant to let their properties because of difficulties ensuring that the tenants vacate when the lease is expired, and the difficulties of ensuring a market for their properties.

The Housing Acts of 1988 and 1996
All new lettings after the 15th January 1989 are governed by the Housing Act 1988, now amended by the Housing Act 1996. This act created two types of tenancy:

- assured tenancy
- shorthold tenancy

For the sake of clarity, they will both be referred to as shorthold tenancies.

Some general principles

The law requires there must be a letting of a dwelling house as a separate dwelling, and:

- it must be let under a lease and not a licence
- the tenant must be an individual, i.e. companies have no protection
- the dwelling must be occupied as the tenant's only or principal home
- it must not be a tenancy specifically excluded from protection of the Act, such as holiday lettings on certain conditions.

Encouraging private lettings under legislation

Under the new legislation all new tenancies are automatically shorthold.

Rent

Regulated rent still applied to most tenancies, which came into existence before the 1988 Act; they were governed by the "fair rent procedure".

The present procedure

The landlord can serve notice on a prescribed form giving notice of a new rent. A notice can be served when the lease expires; alternatively the lease can have included a term for a regular rent increase. If the tenant refers the rent to a rent assessment committee, presently known as the Residential Property Tribunal, it must consider the rent for letting would get in an open market.

Tenancies – regaining possession

- An assured tenancy allows the tenant to remain in the property unless the landlord can show the court he has grounds for possession
- A shorthold tenancy gives minimum security for the tenant, who can be required to leave after six months, provided the landlord has served two months notice.

A shorthold tenancy

This form of tenancy provides the tenant with very little protection. There is no need to give notice stating that a shorthold tenancy is being established, although the landlord must give the terms, commencement date, rent payable etc in writing. The landlord must serve at least two months notice in writing on a tenant to leave the premises and still has to apply to court for an order if the tenant does not leave willingly. A landlord must be granted a court order if a tenant refuses to leave after the expiry of the tenancy. There is no need to prove any of the grounds above.

The main elements

The tenancy may be for a fixed term, e.g. a year less one day or it can run from one rent period to the next. Under normal circumstances the landlord cannot regain his property before the first six months have expired. As a result all tenancies in the private rented sector are now shorthold tenancies unless the landlord has served a notice on the tenant before the beginning of a tenancy that is not intended to be a shorthold tenancy. This has eased the lot of landlords.

Continuing the tenancy – no need for new notice

Shorthold tenancy will continue without any renewal of the agreement.

Excluded tenancies

There are certain excluded tenancies:

- holiday letting of the property
- very high or very low rental properties
- property granted to students

Protection from harassment and eviction

There are two forms of protection:

- criminal prosecution
- civil action for damages

Harassment is any action deliberately intended to make the occupant give up the property or feel too intimidated to exercise his or her legal rights. Examples of harassment include changing of locks, uttering threats, disrupting basic services, accumulating rubbish on the premises and removing light bulbs in common parts.

Assignment and sub-letting
A tenant may be allowed to assign the whole of the remainder of his lease in the tenancy. There may be an absolute prohibition or a qualified prohibition. If it is qualified it is usually with the landlord's consent. Normally the landlord cannot unreasonably withhold consent.

Buying a long leasehold
For the purpose of landlord and tenant law, long leasehold is one that is generally extended for twenty one years or more. A lease for a long leasehold purchase will usually contain expressed terms on the landlord's duties to maintain the premises. The problems may be the landlord has neglected the premises, they have charged an exorbitant amount for necessary works, managing agents do not fulfil their tasks and landlords have carried out unnecessary works.

Buying a freehold
In 1993 an Act was introduced which assisted tenants who wished to buy the freehold of their flats. There is now the Commonhold and Leasehold Reform Act 2002 which amends the qualifications of leaseholders wishing to enfranchise, as well as enhancing their powers to manage their own affairs. The provisions of this Act are not totally in and a public consultation process is in progress about its main provisions.

Long leaseholds – flat dwellers
Under the Leasehold Reform Housing and Urban Development 1993, long leaseholders who qualified are able to acquire the freehold of their premises on certain conditions. This is a group action, for example: two thirds of the flats had to be long leaseholds, at least ninety per cent of the floor space had to be residential, there had to be a low rent, fifty per cent of the leaseholders had to use their flat as their main residence, two thirds of the qualifying tenants occupying at least half of all the flats in the building had to agree to make the purchase. If a block was converted and they had fewer than five flats, there could be no resident landlord on the premises.

Managing agents
Appointment of managing agents
Under the Landlord and Tenant Act 1987, a tenants association may serve notice on the landlord asking to be consulted on the appointment of the managing agents. The whole of the leasehold system is going through reform at the moment.

You and Your Home – Planning
Planning
Although an Englishman's home is his castle, you cannot alter or develop his castle without planning consent from the local authority, and also building regulation approval.

Normally planning consent is related to the land not the person making the application. Therefore if you buy land with an existing planning consent, this consent passes to you the new owner with the land. Usually you local authority is the planning authority.

What sort of development requires planning consent?
Apart from listed buildings and conservation areas, planning law is contained in the Town and Country Planning Act 1990.

If you are building an extension to your home, you make fall within an exemption, which may not require you to apply for planning consent.

When planning consent is given in principal, this gives you some guidance to what the local authority considers acceptable for this particular development.

Development
Development is defined, and you will need planning consent if any development takes place. Development includes carrying out any building, engineering, mining or other operations, in over or under land, making of any material change and use of any buildings, or other land.

Even the demolition of a dwelling house, rebuilding, structural alterations, or additions to a building, that is other operations normally undertaken by a builder are considered to be development, for the purposes of planning regulation.

If however, you are only carrying out works that effect the interior of the buildings, and which do not materially affect the buildings exterior appearance, you will not generally require consent as these activities are not normally considered to be development.

Demolition
Demolition is not normally regarded as being part of development, but may require consent if it relates to a listed building, scheduled monument, building in a conservation area, dwelling house, or building adjacent to a dwelling house, or buildings not exceeding 50 cubic meters in volume.

Change of use
Planning consent may be required if you intend on changing the use of a building.
   Examples of the classifications are:

A1: Shops
A2: Professional Advisors
A3: Food and Drink
B2: General Industrial
B8: Storage and Distribution
C3: Dwelling Houses

The most common is being class C residential use. A dwelling house is defined as a house, that is used as a dwelling, or whether or not sole or main residence by a single person or by people living together as a family, or by not more than six residents living together.
   There is some permitted change between the classes but usually planning permission is needed.
   For instance, A3 is food and drink, and a few years ago Frinton prided itself on never having a Fish and Chip shop until a café which came within the A3 category was able within that category to sell Fish and Chips, much to the shock and horror of the locals.
   Certain forms of development are exempt from planning consent, and these are set out in the Town and Country Planning (General Permitted Development) Order 1995.
   Section 1 and 2 gives consent for certain developments within the curtilage of a dwelling house, and for minor operations. These include such matters as enlarging or improvement, or alteration to the house, additions or alterations to roof only, provision of building including a swimming pool, incidental to the enjoyment of the house, erection of porch and installation of a satellite antenna.
   They may be limited if in fact the property is within a conservation area, or in an area of outstanding natural beauty, or if it is listed.

For instance you can erect, construct, maintain or improve a gate, fence, wall or other means of enclosure, provided they are not more than one metre high if they are adjoining the highway, or two meters in any other case.

Also means of construction to a highway which is not a trunk or classified road.

Further checks.
You may have to check further that you do not require planning consent, that as maybe a special condition on the planning permission that you have already got, and also check that there is what is known as and 'article 4' direction in force which allow the local authority to remove any of the permitted development rights.

Also you need to check your deeds, make sure that there are no restrictions to develop the land, known as a restrictive covenant.

In practise this is one of the most common errors that client's make.

To obtain planning permission and building regulation consent, then when they come to sell the property, the purchasers solicitors finds that they have not obtained permission from the original developer.

If the land is agricultural, you may need to fill in an agricultural holding certificate, because agricultural land is subject to special statutory controls.

Making a planning application
The first port of call is the planning authority, after an informal chat with the planning officer.

Each local authority has its own form of planning application; there are two main types:

- Full
- Outline permission

Outline permission requires a general description of the development and its features, you will need to submit a plan, showing the various boundaries, and if successful, this means that it has been approved in principle.

Once a planning application is made the local authority will give notice to the general public and will consult various organisations about the application, the maybe a site notice or an advert in the local paper or a note just served on adjoining owners.

The decision
The local authority may make three types of decision.

- Refusal
- Permission subject to conditions
- Unrestricted permission

The local authority may grant permission subject to entry into a legal agreement, to carry out certain work or except certain restrictions on the future use of the land, known as a section 106 agreement.
The sort of things that might be involved are:

- Previous planning history of the site
- Access and transport implications
- Environmental considerations
- Impact upon the neighbours

You are likely to get the decision within eight weeks of your application the planning permission runs with the land, so once you get full planning consent, you have to start the building within five years, otherwise the consent has lapsed. If you have outline planning permission you need to ask for approval of the reserved matters within three years of that date. You must being the development within five years of that date of the outline permission or within two years of the approval of the reserved matters. Commencement of the work might be:

- Any construction work
- Demolition Work
- Digging for the foundations
- Laying a pipe, commencing works on a road
- Material change in use of the land.

Section 106 Agreements
These are effectively an agreement that sets the trade-off between local authority and the developer, for the local authority giving its consent. It relates to Section 106 of the Town and Country Planning 1990. It allows the local authority to impose conditions, which would not necessarily be permitted.

Appealing against the refusal of a Planning Permission
The sort of things you can appeal against are:

- failure to give a decision within the original time limit
- Any conditions or refusal of the planning consent.

The appeal
The appeal can either be an enquiry or written representation only.

The vast majority of planning appeals are held by written representations, they are cheaper than having to give oral representations, unlike in legal proceedings, if you lose you appeal you are unlikely to have to pay the winning parties costs from defending the appeal. If you win there is little scope for you to recover you expenses from the local authority, unless you can demonstrate that the local authority acted unreasonably.

Enforcement of Planning Controls
A breach of planning control is not necessarily a criminal offence, because you can in certain circumstances obtain retrospective consent. Usually the time limit for the planning authority to take any action is four years from the date of the project has been completed. In other cases it is ten years.

Usually when the local authorities contemplating enforcing action, they invite you to apply for retrospective planning permission, which if rejected then take enforcement proceedings.

Planning Contravention Notice (PCN)

This sets out in details the alleged breach and the owner or occupier once served has 21 days to respond, if they do not respond, it is a criminal offence.

Injunctions
This is an order by the court that requires the person who is issued to stop the activities that is causing the breach of the planning control. The court has the discretion both to order the injunction and decide on its terms.

Enforcement notice
Once an enforcement notice has been served in respect of a breach, it is a criminal offence. It does not become effective until 28 days after it has been served. It may be suspended while the appeal is going ahead.

BUYING & SELLING YOUR HOME

Stop Notice
The local authority may issue a Stop Notice if the activity is being carried out for more than four years, or if it relates to use of a building as a dwelling house the Stop Notice is not effective.

Breach of Condition Notice
This will set out the steps needed to be taken to ensure with compliance of the planning conditions.

Appealing against an enforcement notice
It is possible to appeal against and enforcement notice on such grounds as:

- Planning permission ought to be granted
- The conditions ought to be discharged
- The matters have not occurred
- The period is unreasonable
- It has been served incorrectly

Compensation
If a Stop Notice is issued and the enforcement notice is either quashed or varied, or withdrawn then compensation is payable.

Conservation Areas
These are obviously to preserve the character of the area. Any building located in a conservation area is subject to the two additional restrictions.

Tree Preservation Orders (TPO's)
This protects a tree or group of trees, which usually comes up on your local search. Which has been carried out prior to the purchase. In 1826 it was decided that a tree was wood applicable to buildings and does not include orchard trees. The size of a tree is not definitive of what is a tree, as it may even be a sapling.
   It is a criminal offence to carry out any works on a tree that is the subject of a TPO, unless you have the local authorities consent.

Listed Buildings
This is a generic term. There are different classes of listed buildings. It is a criminal offence to alter a listed building in a manner, which alters it

character, or historical integrity. There is no defence to plead ignorance. There is no time limit within which the local authority need bring an action for unauthorised works.

Archaeological Finds

The county council has a list of the sites and monuments. The people to contact apart from the local council are English Heritage, the Council for British Archaeology and the Institute of Field Archaeologists.

Building Regulations

Every building project, will need to comply with current building regulations, some local authorities will accept NHBC Buildmark cover as evidence of compliance with building regulations. Building regulations are separate from planning consent and will need to obtain for both. If you fail to comply with the building regulations you may have difficulties in selling your property and you may find yourself at risk from criminal prosecution.

3

CRIMINAL LAW

What is a Crime?
Fundamentally a crime is whatever the state says is a crime. Criminal law is concerned with conduct, which the state considers should be punished, where civil law is concerned with private rights. Crime is a public wrong but conduct, which is harmful to the public, is not necessarily a crime.

Nor is immoral conduct necessarily criminal. A crime therefore can only be defined by reference to procedure "A crime (or offence) is a legal wrong that can be followed by criminal proceedings, which may result in punishment (Glanville Williams)

The Sources of criminal Law
- *The Common Law*
  These are crimes created by the courts these were the system of law that existed even before the Norman Conquest in 1066. The definitions of some of these offences are to be found even today only in case laws e.g. murder, involuntary manslaughter, common assault. It may still be a common law offence even when a later statute sets down the defences or penalties i.e. Homicide Act 1957.

  The courts these days do not have any power to create any more offences these are all set down by act of parliament.
- *The Textbooks.*
  Early legal works such as Coke, Foster, Hawkins, Hale are accepted by the courts as authoritative statements of the law as it stood at the time when the book was written. Modern books may be persuasive e.g. Kenny, Williams, Smith and Hogan.
- *Statute or Act of Parliament.*
  This is the main source of law today, there may be criminal law offences in all sorts of acts not normally thought of as dealing with the criminal law i.e. Income Tax Acts, National Insurance Acts, Health and Safety at work.

- *Subordinate Legislation*
  The act may empower other bodies to pass rules orders or bylaws, which may contain offences. If the ministers or any o these bodies exceed their powers they are said to have acted ultra vires and the rule may be invalid.

Classification of Crimes
- According to source, i.e. as above
- According to method of trial

They are divided in three different ways. The Criminal Law Act 1977 provides as follows:

i) **Indictable offences** – triable in the Crown Court by Judge and Jury only. That is serious offences such as murder, robbery.
ii) **Summary offences** – triable in the Magistrates Court by unpaid, lay or stipendiary magistrates. That is most traffic offences.
iii) **Offences triable either way** – e.g. theft.

It is usual for the defendant to ask if he or she wants to be tried in front of a jury. The Government is trying to cut down on the ability of the defendant to ask to go to the Crown Court for what they regard as minor offences.

- *Treason, arrestable offences, other offences*
  Treason is an offence against the state. Arrestable offences are more serious offences i.e. murder etc.

Criminal Liability

For an act to be a crime it usually requires two elements. The Actus Reus and Mens Rea. This comes from the Latin maxim: actus non-facit reum nisi mens sit rea. This divides into two sections. The actus reus is the physical act, that is the committing of the offence and the mens rea is what we would regard as the guilty mind. Therefore you need to have a guilty mind coupled with a guilty or criminal act.

For the defendant to be found guilty of a criminal offence must be shown that they acted in a particular way, or fail to act in a particular way, or brought about a state of affairs.

There are a considerable number of statutory offences, which only require the act to be proved. These are strict liability offences. Most traffic offences are strict liability and therefore whether or not you intended to carry out the act, you are still guilty. There may also be what is known as a vicarious liability, that is you are liable for the act of another person, an example being allowing someone to drive a vehicle that is not insured, without any MOT and the driver not having a driving licence. The person who allows that act would be guilty vicariously.

Strict Liability

This means that the act itself is criminal and the state of mind of the defendant is unimportant. There is no need to prove a guilty mind.

This is mainly applicable in road traffic offences, where there is a social danger, such as possessing a prohibited weapon. It does not matter that the defendant did not know that he had the weapon.

In all other offences there is a presumption that Mens Rea is required unless statute states otherwise.

A Corporation, which is not a human being, may be held personally liable for acts of its directors or servants. There have been recent cases whereby railway companies have been charged with manslaughter.

Actus Reus

This is the criminal act. This is the conduct, which is forbidden by the rule of the criminal law on the assumption that any necessary mens rea is found to exist. The Actus Reus is what the defendant must have done or failed to have done, and to prove the require Actus Reus it must be shown that the defendant's conduct was voluntary and it occurred while the defendant still had the requisite guilty mind or Mens Rea.

To be voluntary it must be by the person's own free will, and there may be situations whereby they are automatic acts and they may be indefensible automatism which could be allied to say, sleepwalking. There may be sudden physical impairments such a cramp, which could be involuntary.

The person's guilty intent may change, such as appropriating someone's property, deciding later to give it back, and the theft would still have taken place.

In **Fagan v Military Police Commissioner 1969**, a motorist inadvertently drove over a police officer's foot. This was not a guilty act but once it was pointed out that he had done so and he did nothing to change the situation, it then became an assault.

Omissions

Normally to omit to do something is not a guilty act, but there are situations where failure or omission will attract liability where there is a duty to act. Examples are:
   Dangerous situation created by the defendant, and nothing done to resolve it.
   Where a police officer has a duty to intervene to prevent and assault.
   Where the defendant has taken upon himself to do something, and then failed to carry out. Such as a failure to look after some mentally ill person.
   In circumstances where the defendant is in charge of a young person, in a parental relationship.

There has to be shown there has to be a cause between the acts and the consequences that would not have happened but for the defendants act or omission.

There may be intervening acts, which would cause a link to be broken.

In drug cases for instance, it might be said that the drug dealers that supply the drug caused the death of the person, but unless the drug dealer actually administers the drug the drug dealer is unlikely to held liable for the causing death.

In the eggshell skull cases the defendants must take their victims as they find them, so if the victim has a particularly thin skull or is of a nervous disposition, that is the defendant's bad luck.

The various parties may have different degrees of involvement, such as either a principal or an accessory.

A principal is one who carried out all the requirements for that particular offence, and an accessory is someone who helped or brought about the commission of the offence.

The accessory may aid, abet, counsel or procure the offence.

The words aid, abet, counsel or procure are generally used together and without separate definition applying to each word, but they generally mean aiding, which is giving help support or assistance. Abetting, inciting, instigating or encouraging. Counselling would mean either advising or instructing and procuring would mean bringing about.

Corporate Liability

Corporations have a separate legal personality of their own, and they can won property, employ people and bring lawsuits. But cannot commit offences.

A company OLL Ltd has been convicted through its managing director of manslaughter following the school canoing tragedy at Lyme Bay in 1994.

Vicarious Liability
This is usually when an employee breaches a statutory duty as part of their employment.
The sort of things that would be a criminal act are:

- A physical act such as a blow
- Words such as in incitement, conspiracy, blackmail.
- An omission, where there is a legal duty to do something
- Possession as in drug offences
- A state of affairs as in being found in a dwelling house for an unlawful purpose
- Conduct of others in vicarious liability

Mens rea
This is usually an intention or recklessness. It is necessary to distinguish them since some crimes require nothing less than intention, i.e. an attempt and wounding with intent. Therefore the act doesn't have to be carried out, as in a conspiracy.

- *Intention* – this has to be a desire or purpose
- *Recklessness* – this is where the consequence of the action is not desired but the person knows there is a risk an event may result from his conduct, or that a circumstance may exist and he takes that risk.

Attempt
It is an offence of Common Law to attempt to commit any indictable offence or an offence triable either way. You have to have the mens rea for an attempt, recklessness is not sufficient. Attempted murder requires the intention to kill. The attempt must go beyond mere preparation.

Negligence
Negligence is when someone does not comply with the standards of reasonableness.
These focus on the defendant's conduct rather that their state of mind.
Negligence still has some flavour of fault or blame, and the defendant must be shown to have acted in a less than reasonable way.
In recent years the court has tried to develop an idea of corporate manslaughter, they have to prove that an individual person was negligent.

The statutes have used different ways to describe various states of mind, such as:
Intent, recklessness, wilfully, dishonestly and these have developed there own definitions.

Intent
In case of burglary for instance, under the Theft Act 1968, a burglar must have intention to enter the house as a trespasser, intending to steal property, whether or not the defendant intended particular consequence will be q question of fact left tot he jury or the magistrates.

Recklessness
There is no all-purpose definition of recklessness, and the test will generally be subjective.

Wilfully
The defendant must be shown to have desired the consequences of his or her actions, and at least have foreseen them.
Wilful can also mean that the act was voluntary.

Dishonestly
This is important in the Theft Acts 1968–1978. The defendant must be shown to have acted dishonestly.

Robinson (1915)
A jeweller was held not guilty of attempting to obtain false pretences when he staged a fake robbery. He was going to claim against the insurance but he had not claimed therefore there was no attempt. Today he would have been charged with wasteful employment of the police.

In the past we had a situation whereby you could even attempt the impossible i.e. attempting to steal from the pocket which was in fact empty. Under the Criminal Attempts Act 1981, the Act provides that a person may be guilty of attempting to commit an offence even though the facts were such that the commission of the offence would have been impossible.

Burden of proof
The burden of proof in criminal matters is beyond reasonable doubt. In some cases it may be on balance of probabilities, that is the civil burden of proof e.g. insanity diminished responsibility.

Offences against the person
These are:

Murder:
The defence is a person of sound memory and of the age of discretion unlawfully kills any reasonable creature with malice aforethought. The definition of a reasonable creature means a human being not a foetus, as it does not become a person until it has an existence independent of the mother.

The year and a day rule, whereby if death occurs more than a year and a day after injury it was not unlawful homicide, was abolished in 1966. In homicide causation problems can arise. The defendant will only be liable if the act was a substantial cause of the death. In **Jordan (1956)** the injured person died a few days after being given an antibiotic. The Court of Appeal decided that the cause of death was the negligent treatment, not the wound.

The malice aforethought for murder was traditionally regarded as:

- Intention to kill
- Intention to cause grievous bodily harm
- Recklessness as to death

Famous case of **Moloney (1985)** where the defendant and his stepfather both being drunk, decided to challenge each other to load and fire a shotgun. The defendant fired without aiming and blew the stepfather's head off. He admitted manslaughter but maintained that he had no foresight whatsoever of the possibility of death or injury to his victim. The House of Lords decided he should be acquitted of murder as in his drunken state he might have failed to foresee death or injury at all, and that only intent to kill or cause serious harm would suffice for malice aforethought.

Defences to murder are the execution of justice, self defence, prevention of violence or if the death was accidental.

Manslaughter
There are two types of manslaughter:

- *Voluntary manslaughter*
  Has to have malice aforethought, but not murder if:
  i) *Provocation*. Provocation has to be any act, which would cause any reasonable person to have the sudden and temporary loss of self-control,

rendering the accused so subject to passion as to make them for the moment not masters of their minds.

A reasonable man is one of the same age and characteristics as the accused. The loss of self-control must be sudden and temporary and there should not be a considerable delay.

ii) *Diminished responsibility.* Under the Homicide Act 1957 where a person kills or is a party to the killing of another they shall not be convicted of murder if they are suffering from abnormality of the mind.

iii) *Killing in the course of a suicide pact.* This shall be manslaughter not murder for a person acting in pursuance of a suicide pact between him and another to kill the other, or to is party to the other being killed by a third person. Obviously the defendant has to prove that there was such a pact. Although under the Suicide Act 1961, suicide is no longer a crime, it is a crime to aid, abet, counsel or procure the suicide of another or an attempt of another to commit suicide.

iv) *Excessive self-defence.* If the defendant in self-defence kills by using more force than is allowed, the defendant is entitled to a verdict of manslaughter not murder.

- *Involuntary manslaughter.*
  There appear to be three types:
  i) *Killing by gross negligence.* Must show such disregard for life and safety of others as to amount to crime against the State.
  ii) *Killing by intentionally doing an unlawful and dangerous act.* (Constructive manslaughter.) The act must not only be unlawful it must be dangerous.
  iii) *Killing by an intentional act,* being reckless whether the bodily harm less than grievous bodily harm results

Infanticide

Under section 1 of the Infanticide Act 1938 provides where a woman causes the death of her child under the age of twelve months but at the time the balance of her mind was disturbed by reason of her not having fully recovered from the effect of giving birth to the child, she shall be guilty of infanticide not murder, and dealt with as manslaughter.

Causing death by dangerous driving

Parliament provided for the offence of causing death by dangerous driving with an objective test for danger.

CRIMINAL LAW

Child destruction and abortion
It is not murder to kill a child in the womb or while being born. The most important Act being the Abortion Act 1967. Medical termination of the pregnancy is protected if two medical practitioners are of the opinion that continuance of the pregnancy would involve risk to the mother's life or injury to her physical or mental health.

Assault and battery
There are two distinct offences. Assault is any act by which the defendant intentionally or recklessly causes the other person to fear immediate unlawful personal violence. Battery is intentional or reckless infliction of unlawful personal violence. The courts however, often use assault to cover both. It is possible to assault without physically touching them i.e. threats down the telephone. The defences might be lawful physical chastisement by parents on their children or by schoolteachers in respect of children at school, also self-defence.

As previously mentioned Assault – causing another person to apprehend immediate or unlawful personal violence. Battery is application of force. The smallest amount of force would be sufficient and can be applied directly or indirectly. The state of mind of the victim is relevant. The victim must apprehend immediate use of unlawful force, so even if imitation firearms were used the victim would be assaulted if he or she believed that the firearm was real.

Even words can be an assault, such as threats down the telephone; even silent could fulfil the requirements if the victim thought he was in fear of unlawful force.

They can be conditional threats, as in the case of **Tuberville v Savage 1669**.

Lawful Chastisement
Those acting in *loco parentis* may be able to use reasonable force in controlling the behaviour of that child.

This is currently undergoing a large change, where almost no force may now be applied to children.

Assault occasioning actual bodily harm
Section 47 of the Offences against the Person Act 1861. The harm need not be serious but there must be some harm e.g. bruising. In the **R v. Ireland (1996)** silent phone calls were held to be capable of constitution assault occasioning actual bodily harm. In **R v. Burstow (1996)** the defendant made

silent phone calls to his victim and sent her hate mail, as a result of which she suffered severe depression. Therefore a stalker can be convicted under this section even if he has not applied physical violence either directly or indirectly.

Malicious wounding
Section 20 of the Offences against the Person Act 1861. It is an offence unlawfully and maliciously to wound or inflict any grievous bodily harm upon any other person. Grievous means really serious, malicious means intentionally or recklessly.

Wounding with intent
Unlawfully and maliciously to wound or cause any bodily harm to any person with intent to do some grievous bodily harm to any person. Wounding means to break two layers of skin, there must be a break in the skin.

Administering poison
Section 23 and 24 of the same Act provides two offences of administering poison.

Assault on, resistance to, or obstruction of a police constable in the execution of his or her duty
Protection from harassment
The Protection from Harassment Act 1997 makes it an offence to pursue a cause of conduct amounting to harassment of a person or gives them cause to fear that violence will be used against them.

Firearms and offensive weapons
It is an offence to carry offensive weapons in public places without lawful authority or reasonable excuse. This was extended to a sawn-off shotgun was left in a locked car. Reasonable excuse may be self-defence but it must be of an imminent particular threat. It was ruled that the possession of a prohibited weapon was an offence of strict liability.

Sexual offences
Under the Sexual Offences Act 1956 the offences include:

- *Rape. Sexual Offences Act 2003, Section 1*
  This in triable on indictment and maximum penalty of life imprisonment.

It has been extended now to cover penetration of the vagina, mouth or anus of the victim, in proving rape you must show that the victim did not in fact consent at the time and the defendant did not reasonably believe he or she consented.

The reasonableness of the defendant's belief is determined having regard to all the circumstances. The question of consent is a question of fact. The facts of a rape are easier to prove than the intentions and the wishes of the victim at the time.

Unlawful sexual intercourse with a woman who at the time does not consent, and at that time he knows she does not consent or he has reckless as to whether she consents or not. It is now agreed that in our **R v. R (1991)** the husband was convicted of attempting to rape his wife on the basis that all non-consensual sexual intercourse, even in marriage is unlawful. The Sexual Offences Act 1993 abolished the assumption of criminal law that a boy under the age of 14 is incapable of sexual intercourse.

- *Intercourse with girls under 16.*
  Intercourse with a girl under 13 is punishable with life imprisonment. Consent is no defence, nor is reasonable belief the girl is over 13. Intercourse with a girl under 16 carries a penalty of two years imprisonment.
- *Incest*
  It is an offence for a man to have sexual intercourse with a woman he knows to be his granddaughter, daughter, sister or mother. Corresponding offence for a woman in respect of her grandfather, father, brother or son. Consent is no defence.
- *Sexual Assault*
  This replaces the old indecent assault
  This is now broken down into assault by penetration
  Assault by touching, causing sexual activity without consent.
  Sexual activity in the presence of a child
  Causing a child to watch a sex act
  Arranging intended child sex offences
  Meeting a child following sexual grooming – *Sexual Offences Act 2003, Sect 15*
  Abuse of Position of Trust – *Sexual Offences Act 2003, sections 16–19*

The new offences are far wider and relate to offences of a sexual activity with a child by a person in a position of trust.

Protection of Children – Criminal Justice and Court Services Act 2000
Due to a number of measures aimed at preventing unsuitable people working with children, disqualification orders were introduced, and these order were aimed at disqualifying people who presented a threat to children from working in certain jobs and positions.

The court must impose these when defendants are convicted or certain offences, these include:
The defendant being over 18 and is convicted of an offence against a child
The offence consists of physical or psychic assault accompanied by circumstances of indecency.

- *Indecency with children.*
Any person who commits an offence of gross indecency with or towards a child under the age of 14, or incites a child under that age to such an act, is guilty of an offence.
- *Protection of children.*
The Protection of Children Act 1999 identifies individuals who are unsuitable to work with children.
- *Notification of sex offenders.*
Part 1 of the Sex Offenders Act 1997 requires persons convicted or cautioned in respect of certain sex offences to notify the police of their names and addresses.
- *Sexual acts abroad.*
In accordance with Part 2 of the Sex Offenders Act 1997 it is an offence for a British citizen to commit certain sexual acts abroad against children
- *Abuse of a position of trust.*
It is an offence for a person aged 18 or over to have sexual intercourse or any other sexual activity with, or directed towards such a person if he is in a position of trust in relation to that other person.

Offences against property
Offences under the Theft Act 1968. – section 1
This is triable either way and the maximum or seven year's imprisonment on indictment, or six month imprisonment and/or a summary fine
There are five key elements to the offence of theft, they are:

- Dishonesty
- Appropriation
- Property

- Belonging to another
- Intention of permanently depriving

The definition is that theft is dishonestly appropriating property belonging to another with the intention of permanently depriving the other of it. The actus reus is appropriating property belonging to another, so stealing can happen even if the person comes by it innocently and then later assumes the rights, such as a bailee, that is a person to whom items have been left, then decides to sell it. Switching labels on a supermarket item is theft.

There are exceptions for what is known as a bona fide purchaser for value. To be stolen property must belong to another, thus abandoned property cannot be stolen nor can it be if the person believes it to be abandoned. Another definition of property belonging to any person is that that person has possession or control of it, or having in it any proprietary right or interest, therefore the owner can steal from someone with a lesser prior interest, e.g. a bailee. In Rose v. Matt (1951) the defendant pawned his clock and then retrieved it when the broker was not looking and was convicted of what would now be theft.

Section 2 does not define dishonesty but a person is not dishonest if he had a belief that he has in law the right to deprive the other of it, or that he would have the others consent if the other knew, or if the person to whom the property belongs cannot be discovered by taking reasonable steps, i.e. finding lost property.

It is left to the Jury as to whether someone is dishonest. In Feeley (1972) the manager of a shop against the rules, takes money from the till knowing that it can be repaid within a few days.

Appropriates
Section 3 states:

> Any assumption of the rights of an owner amounts to an appropriation. Thus this includes coming by the property innocently without stealing it and later assuming the right of it by keeping or dealing with it as its owner.

Property
The Theft Act 1968 Section 4 states:

> The property includes money and all property real or personal including things in action, and other intangible property.

Things in action can include patents and trademarks and other things, which can only be enforced by legal action as opposed to physical possession. It could include software programmes, confidential information,
New offences are being created so that:
Mobile telephones (Reprogramming) Act 2002. This is due to the high percentage of mobile phones stolen over recent years to try and reduce their attractiveness to thieves.

Cheques – these are known as things in action
Land – you cannot generally steal land, even though it is property for the purposes of criminal damage.
Certain things are 'not property'.

Human bodies are not property, although the Court of Appeal in *Crown v Kelly (1999)* upheld convictions of two people involved in a theft of body parts from the Royal College of Surgeons.

The court said that it was theft on the grounds of the process of alteration in which the body parts had undergone did make them 'property'

Belonging to another
That is any one who has possession or control of it.

Intention of Permanently Depriving
This occurs when the person intends to treat the thing as his own; to dispose of regardless of the other's rights, and borrowing or lending of it may amount to so treating.

So if someone borrowed a season ticket causing the owner to miss a match it is an outright taking.

Robbery – Theft Act 1968
Section 8
Section 8. Robbery is stealing and immediately before or at the time of doing so and in order to do so, using force on any person or putting or seeking to put any person in fear of being then and there subject to force. The penalty is life imprisonment. If there is no theft there is no robbery. For example in **Skivington (1968)** the defendant went to his sister's firm to collect wages due to her. When the cashier refused he threatened the cashier with a knife. Held it was not robbery because the defendant had a claim of right.

CRIMINAL LAW

Burglary Theft Act 1968
Section 9
Section 9. Entering a building or an inhabited vehicle or vessel as a trespasser with intent to steal, to inflict grievous bodily harm, to rape or do unlawful damage, and having entered, steals or carries out the above. Aggravated burglary is if at the time of the burglary he has with a firearm or imitation firearm, any weapon of offence or any explosive.

Aggravated Burglary Theft Act 1968
Section 10
If a person commits any burglary and at the time has with him any firearm of imitation firearm

Taking a motor vehicle or other conveyance without authority – Theft Act 1968
Section 12
Allowing yourself to be carried:

If you cannot prove who took the vehicle, you must be able to show that the defendant allowed him or herself to be carried in it.

The other occupants in the vehicle can be charged, provided there is sufficient evidence.

Colloquially known as "twocing", can also be an offence to allow yourself to be carried in such a vehicle.

Abstracting of electricity – Theft Act 1968
Section 13
Electricity cannot be stolen, it is an offence to dishonestly use without due authority any electricity.

A person who dishonestly uses without authority or dishonestly causes to be wasted or diverted any electricity shall be guilty of an offence.

Electricity is not property; a specific offence was created to deal with this.

Handling stolen Goods – Theft Act 1968 – Section 22
This happens if a person knowing or believing them to be stolen, dishonestly receives the goods or dishonestly undertakes or assists in there retention, removal, disposal or realisation, by or for the benefit of another person, or if he arranges to do so.

This can be difficult to prove, if someone just asks no questions.

Obtaining property by deception
In this case the owner has voluntarily handed over the property. In R. v. Preddy (1996) the House of Lords said that as no identifiable property passes between two bank account by cheque or by telegraphic or electronic transfer, then the payee cannot be guilty of dishonesty. There has been on amendment in 1996 of obtaining a money transfer by deception.

Obtaining a pecuniary advantage by deception
Such as borrowing by way of overdraft or taking out a policy of insurance or earns extra remuneration. In **Callender (1992)** the defendant was convicted of pretending to hold accountancy qualifications.

False accounting
Section 17. Where a person dishonestly, with a view to gain for himself or another or with intent to cause loss to another, destroys, defaces, conceals or falsifies accounts.

Blackmail
Section 21
Person makes an unwarranted demand with menaces.
Handling stolen goods
Penalty 14 years, higher than the penalty for theft. It is when a person knowing or believing them to be stolen, dishonestly receives the goods or undertakes or assists in their retention, removal, disposal or realisation. In Pitchley (1973) when the person knew the money had been stolen he did nothing about it. He was guilty of assisting and retaining.

Making off without payment
It is an offence for a person, knowing that payment on the spot for any goods is required, dishonestly makes off without having paid or required, or expected to and with intent to avoid payment.

Criminal damage
Criminal Damage Act. Without lawful excuse to destroying or damaging any property belonging to another, intentionally or recklessly. Damage may be slight but there must be some perceptible, physical harm. In **A (a juvenile) (1978)** a football supporter spat on a constable's raincoat. The prosecution argued that it must have been damaged because it needed dry cleaning. It was

held the raincoat is not damaged in this way, although for a satin wedding dress might have been.

Lloyd v. D.P.P. (1992) D damaged a clamp placed on his car unlawfully parked in a private car park. It was held he committed criminal damage, as he had no right to damage or destroy the clamp. **Smith** (1974) the defendant wrongly believed that wiring which he had installed in his flat belonged to him, and removed it when he left. In law it had become a landlord's fixture. Held: honest belief that the property was his own was a defence.

Forgery
Is a false instrument in order that may be used as a genuine one. **Gold v. Schifreen** (1987) Gained illicit access to a database obtained by using someone else's identity number. Held not forgery but now it might be an offence under the Computer Misuse Act 1990.

Trespass
Squatting has caused problems in order to give some legal protection against it. Five offences are enacted on the Criminal Law Act 1977. Section 6, it is an offence for any person without lawful authority to use or threaten violence for the purpose of securing entry into any premises for himself or another, provided that there is someone present on those premises at the time he is opposed to the entry.

Unlawful eviction and harassment of a residential occupier
This is made an offence under section 1 of the Protection from Eviction Act 1977.

Other offences
Bigamy
This is under the Offences against the Person Act 1861, provides that whosoever being married, shall marry any other person during the life of the former husband or wife, whether the marriage shall have taken place in England, Wales or elsewhere. The defendant's reasonable belief that the spouse was dead shall be a defence, even though there had not been seven years absence.

Road traffic offences

Careless driving.
It is an offence to drive a motor vehicle on a road without due care and attention. The standard is objective and is the same for learner drivers as is for experienced ones. Is the accused exercising the degree of care, attention a reasonable and prudent driver would exercise in the circumstances.

Inconsiderate driving.
I.e. driving too slowly, driving through a puddle splashing pedestrians, dangerous driving, a person who drives on a road recklessly should be guilty of an offence, causing death by dangerous driving.

Driving under the influence of drink.
In charge of a motor vehicle is unfit to drive through drink or drugs. Driving with the blood alcohol concentration above the prescribed limit.

Control of dangerous dogs.
The Dangerous Drugs Act 1997 provides for criminal penalties against the owners of any breed of dog, which acts in a dangerous fashion.

Prevention of Terrorism.
The Prevention of Terrorism Act 2000.

Prevention of violence or disorder at football matches.
Assisting arrestable offenders, concealing an arrestable offence, causing wasteful employment of the police, computer misuse and misuse of telecommunications system.

Criminal Injuries Compensation Board.
Established in 1964. Must be shown the injury is one for which the Courts would award compensation of at least £150. About 12,500 applications are made yearly to the board.

4

YOU AND YOUR NEIGHBOURS
Civil Law – The Law of Tort

The word "tort" comes from the Latin tortus meaning crooked or twisted, and the Norman-French tort, meaning wrong. In English law we use the word tort to denote certain civil wrongs as distinct from criminal wrongs. In the middle Ages it was developed that certain wrongs were anti-social to the King – treason, murder, theft, arson and the like, and were offences against the King's peace. The King and the State disregarded other wrongs, and these were left to be reinforced by the person claiming to be injured or wronged. The claim if any was for damages i.e. money compensation or reparation for the injury inflicted by the defendant. The most important civil wrong in medieval society was trespass. This was available for all direct injuries to the person, goods or land.

The nature of a tort
- ***The distinction between a tort and a crime:***
  A crime is the object of criminal proceedings and there is going to be punishment. The object of proceedings in tort is not punishment but compensation or reparation. The same facts may disclose a crime and a tort, therefore in theft there may be a crime of theft and trespass to the goods. That is a tort of conversion. If X assaults Y there is both a crime and a tort.
- ***Breach of contract:***
  Contracts are fixed by the parties themselves, but in a tort the duties are fixed by law and arise by the operation of law itself.
- ***Breach of trust:***
  Although compensation may be awarded for damages suffered by reason of breach of trust, the real distinction is due to the history of equity and common law rather than to logical reasons and development.

Definition of a tort
A tort is a civil wrong for which the remedy is a common law action for unliquidated damages and which is not exclusively the breach of a contract or the breach of trust, or merely equitable obligation.

Damage and liability
Where one person suffers harm or damage at the hands of another, then action in tort for that damage or injury arises, i.e. where A negligently collides with B's stationary car we may find a situation where there is no legal remedy, such as where a giant supermarket sets up a adjacent to, and in competition with a small family grocer, harm is done to the grocer but there is no remedy.

Malice
In tort the intention or motive for the action is generally irrelevant. General defences in tort are:

- **Volenti non-fit injuria.**
("No injury can be done to a willing person"). Examples being in sport – the consent of the player must be true consent to both the physical and legal risk. It may be expressed orally or in writing or may be implied. Mere knowledge of a risk is not usually sufficient; there must be consent to the risk.

  The defence does not apply where a dangerous situation has been created by the defendant's negligent action and a person is placed in an emergency to decide to act to save or protect the life of others or the defendant. A person of reasonable courage who acts and is injured in these circumstances cannot be described as acting willingly.

  In Haynes v. Harwood (1935). The Plaintiff, a constable, was injured stopping defendant's horse, which had bolted due to defendant's negligence. Held: that the defendant was liable in negligence while the plaintiff, who was doing his duty, was not contributory negligent.

  Accidents on the highway show an important application of the doctrine of Volenti. Road users may expect to run the risk of pure accident but not injury due to carelessness. In an early car case, Dann v. Hamilton (1939) it was held the defendant had knowledge of a potential danger and was aware of H's state of inebriation when accepting the lift, she was held not to have assented to his negligent driving.

  Nowadays under Section 148 of the Road Traffic Act 1972, prevents the

defence of Volenti non fit injuria succeeding against a passenger suing a driver in these circumstances, but the claimant's knowledge of the driver's state is treated as contributory negligence. In Owens v. Brimmell (1976) where 20% was deducted from the damages.
- *Mistake.*
Mistake of law is no defence in tort. Ignorance of the law is no excuse. As to mistake of fact, there are exceptions to the rule. It must be a reasonable mistake and may afford a defence.
- *Necessity.*
In some cases damage done intentionally may be excused if done from necessity. The defence is a rare one and is available only if the defendant was compelled by the circumstances to prevent a greater evil. Leigh v. Gladstone (1909). A suffragette went on a hunger strike; she was forcibly fed and later sued for assault and battery. Held: that the defence of necessity was good.
- *Self-defence.*
A person may use reasonable force to defend him or herself against unlawful force. Must be proportionate to the harm threatened. An occupier of property may protect that property by using reasonable means e.g. barbed wire fencing. Spring guns may not be set to injure trespassers who come to the property, nor may a shot be fired at them for such an amount of force is not proportionate to the harm or threat.

Capacity of parties

You must have the capacity to sue and be sued for a tort and this is generally anyone of full age.

- *The Crown*
Until 1947 it was the King can do no wrong but under the Crown Proceedings Act 1947, the Crown is now subject to the law of torts as in cases committed by its servants and agents. The Queen may not be sued in her private capacity.
- *Judicial immunity.*
Judges have absolute immunity for acts within their judicial capacity. This applies to magistrates counsel and witnesses relating to the case with which they are concerned.
- *Foreign sovereigns and diplomats*
These extend to members of their families and to some employees, see parking tickets in London.

- *Corporations*
  It can sue and be sued in its corporate name. It is liable vicariously for torts committed by its servants or agents acting within the scope of their authority.
- *Trade Unions.*
  These are unincorporated bodies protected by the Trade Union Act 1984. To ensure immunity a ballot must be held prior to a strike.
- *Infants or minors.*
  Minority is no defence in tort. The infant may however not have the capacity if some form of intention is necessary. An unborn child may sue.

  Parents are not liable merely because they are parents but will be liable where there has been authorisation or commissioning or ordering of the tort. A parent permitted his son aged 15 to remain in possession of a shotgun of which complaints had been made. The father was then liable for injury. If the parent took reasonable precautions and could not foresee the injury then he was not liable.
- *Persons of unsound mind.*
  They are liable for their torts but they like minors may be unable to form an intention.
- *Married women.*
  At common law a husband could not sue his wife in tort and vice versa except for the protection and security of her own property. Now each may sue the other under a 1962 act for instance in car cases.
- *Aliens.*
  Enemy aliens cannot bring an action in tort. Other aliens have neither disability nor immunity.

Remoteness of damage
This is the neighbour principle and is restricted by:

- Test of directness
- The test of reasonable foresight.

Another important principle is the eggshell skull cases. That is you take your victim as you find them so even if the plaintiff had a thin skull you are still liable.

Vicarious liability in tort
Where A instructs another as in master and servant, and the liability for the principal for the torts of an independent contractor.

- ## Master and servant.
  The master is liable for acts committed during the course of their employment and covers wrongful acts or omissions expressly or impliedly authorised, an unauthorised act which is authorised by the master and something which is ratified by the master.

  With an independent contractor the principal is liable only for the torts which the contractor has been expressly or impliedly authorised to commit.

  The other important tests are who is a servant and the course of employment. In Harrison v. Michelin Tyre Co Ltd (1985), a practical joke injured a fellow employee. The employers argued he was on a frolic of his own.

  The court decided that what he did was in the course of his employment and were therefore liable. Both are liable but usually the master is more worth suing.

Trespass
Three types of trespass – to the person, to the goods and to land.

Assault, battery and false imprisonment
This is an act, which causes another person to apprehend immediate and unlawful violence. Mere words do not constitute an assault. In Tuberville v. Savage (1969) a person laid a hand on their sword and said "If it were not assize time, I would not take such language from you". This was held not to be an assault.

Battery
Force however slight to the person of another. Examples would include a black eye, throwing water at them, holding them by the arm, spitting in their face.

Volenti not fit injuria might be a defence, that is they consented. It must be intentional or negligent.

False imprisonment.
Infliction of bodily restraint of another without lawful justification. It is actionable without proof of damage. The mere holding of an arm may be sufficient.

Stay there or I will shoot you may be evidence. The imprisonment has to be total and if the plaintiff can go another way then he is not imprisoned.

The following defences may be offered to an action for trespass to the person

Self defence
It is lawful to defend yourself against and assault or battery. It must be proportionate to the attack.

Defence of property
An occupier may use reasonable force to eject a trespasser.

Consent of claimant as in Volenti
Parental or other authority.
A parent may administer reasonable punishment to a child or young person. i.e. locking them in their room.

Judicial authority
i.e. An arrest warrant.

Preservation of the peace.
Everyone owes a duty not to disturb the public peace by committing crime or causing public disorders. A constable may only use reasonable force.

Protection from harassment
Protection from Harassment Act 1997 a person must have fear of violence against them there may be a restraining order.

Trespass to land
It may take three forms entry on the land or another, remaining on the land and placing or throwing any material object upon the land of another.

It is not necessary to prove damage it is a tort per se. The sign trespasser may be prosecuted is not true. Mere trespass on land is not a crime and no prosecution for it may be brought. It is accompanied by damage i.e. by breaking fences or treading down growing corn may be criminal damage. Mistake for trespass is no defence.

Where permission has expired i.e. the end of licence they may become trespassers.

Justification or entry.
- lawful authority i.e. police to make an arrest or search or by bailiffs
- entry to abate a nuisance or emergency
- entry to take a chattel owned by defendant
- entry by licence or permission
- peaceable entry on the land by a person entitled to possession

Remedies for trespass to land
- damages
- injunctions
- ejection

Trespass to goods
Trespass is essentially a wrong of possession as distinct from ownership.

Interference with goods.
Detinue means the wrongful detention of the goods or another to the immediate possession of which that other is entitled. I.e. a lent book is not returned.

Conversion is the act of depriving the other of the use and possession of it.

Nuisance
A pubic nuisance is some unlawful act or omission, which endangers or interferes with the lives safety or comfort of the public generally examples are keeping a brothel, obstructing the public highway, excessive smoke fumes or dirt.

A public nuisance is a crime a private person may also sue.

Statutory nuisance public health, clean air, noise abatement, pollution poisonous wastes

Private nuisance causing material injury to property or sensible personal discomfort.

These include rights of way, rights of support, and rights of support of land.

Other nuisances are noise, vibrations, fumes, smell, smoke, dirt and damp, some damage must have occurred.

The following defences are ineffectual:

- That the claimant came to the nuisance. It has to be reasonable in that locality

- That the particular act is for the public benefit
- That all care and skill have been used to prevent the nuisance.

Remedies, abatement, damages and injunction.
Negligence
This is one of the most important and common torts in the law. It was developed in the 19th Century and exists in its own right as a separate and independent tort.
It means:

- a state of mind e.g. where A commits a trespass through inadvertence or carelessness and
- an independent tort

The claimant must prove three things
- that the defendant was under a duty of care to the plaintiff
- that there had been a breach of that duty of care
- that as a result the plaintiff has suffered damage

The Duty of Care.
If you owe no duty you can be as negligent as you please to the whole world. Therefore you can do what you like on your own land as long as if affects no one else.
  When does a duty arise? You owe a duty of care to all other road users. Doctors owe a duty to patients, employers to work colleagues, teachers to students. The list is endless. "The categories of negligence are never Closed Lord Macmillan in Donoghue v Stevenson.

Donoghue v Stevenson (1932)
On of the most famous cases in English law along with Carlill and the Carbolic Smoke Ball Company.
  A friend bought a bottle of ginger beer manufactured by the defendant. The plaintiff became ill from the contents it is alleged that it contained a decomposed snail.
  The House of Lords Held that the manufacturer owed a duty of care to the ultimate consumer.
  The consumer had no cause of action in contract, as she hadn't bought it. Lord Atkin said

- You must take reasonable care to avoid acts of omissions, which you can reasonably foresee would be likely to injure your neighbour.
- Who is my neighbour? Those who are closely affected your actions the rule applies to food, clothing, hair-dyes and similar matters.

Recognised duties in law
- Highways other road user also applies to railways, shipping and canal navigation. There is no duty of care for highway authorities to promote safety of road users.
- Employers liability. An employer owes a duty of care to employees to provide a safe system of work, reasonably safe machinery and competent fellow employees.

Pape v Cumbria CC (1992)
The mere provision of gloves did not discharge the duty of care when the employee contracted dermatitis they had to instruct and encourage her towards them

- Professional Persons
- All the usual professionals

Anns v L.B. of Merton (1977)
A local authority passed defective foundations as safe and owed a duty to owners and occupiers who might suffer. But in Murphy v Brentwood District Council (1990) it was overruled and a local authority was not liable in negligence to an owner or occupier where the costs of remedying dangerous defect results from the negligent failure of the local authority to control the building inspection.

- Carriers

Duty of care to passengers
- Schools Duty of care to the children and those injured by the children
- Police Owed to the general public but not to an individual in respect of losses caused by their failure to apprehend criminals.

Smoldon v Whitworth (1996)
A rugby referee was held liable to the players to protect them form the unnecessary and dangerous aspects of the game.

In Munroe V London Fire and civil defence authority (1996) it was held that on the grounds of public policy that the fire brigade in not under a common-law duty of care in carrying out its fire fighting functions.

The Standard of Care.
Contributory negligence
Before 1945 a defendant could escape liability by showing that the accident wouldn't have happened had no the claimant contributed to his or her own negligence. The damages will be reduced to such extent as the court thinks just and equitable having regard to the claimants share in the responsibility for the damage.

Surveyors were not totally liable is the lender had an imprudent lending policy.

Doctrine of novus actus interveniens
A new act intervening between the wrongful act or omissions.

Sayers v Harlow UDC (1958)
Plaintiff locked in public lavatory she could not get out; she hurt herself as she climbed out. She balanced on a revolving toilet roll and she was one third negligent.

Not wearing a seat belt 25 per cent contributory negligence

Breach of statutory duty
A right may exist in tort because of a breach of an act such as Health and safety at work act 1974

Death survival of actions

Usually a personal action dies with the person. Fatal accidents Act 1846 allow dependants to recover damages if they have suffered financial loss.

Occupiers Liability
Occupiers Liability Act 1957 any one who comes onto premises is a visitor and a safe environment must be provided.

Defences
The visitor was warned, consent that the occupier employed a competent independent contractor.

Trespassers
An occupier has no active duty to trespasses but may not create dangers intentionally.

Children
The copier must be prepared that children will be less careful. You have to be careful to lure children i.e. turntables, poisons berries electric railway lines.

The rule in Rylands v Fletcher (1868)
A person who for his own purposes brings on his lands and collects and keeps there anything likely to do mischief if it escapes must keep it in at his peril and he does no do so prima facie answerable for all the damage which is the natural consequence of its escape

Water from a reservoir flooded plaintiff's mines.

It is one of strict liability

It relates to various types of escape such as electricity, yew tress, wire fencing, sewage and explosives. Some damage must be proved.

Defences, act of God, act of a stranger, default of the claimant, consent of claimant, statutory authority.

Defamation
Defamation is the publication of a statement, which exposes a person to hatred, ridicule or contempt or causes them to be shunned or avoided by right-thinking members of society generally. In other words it is a false statements about a person to their discredit. Libel is in permanent from a slander, which is transitory.

Permanent may be written printed statement, an effigy, and a statue a picture or a film. Libel if it tends to be breach of the peace is a crime whereas slander as such is not. Libel is actionable per se no loss has to be shown.

In slander the claimant must prove actual damage except in the following cases imputation of a crime that is punishable by imprisonment, imputation that the claimant is suffering from a contagious disease i.e. VD, imputation of unchastity in a woman this includes lesbianism and unfitness for office i.e. a solicitor knows no law or a carpenter that they cannot make a simple joint.

Tolley v Fry (1931)
Defendants published a picture of a golfer with a packet of their chocolate in his pocket. This suggested he was taking their money and affecting his amateur status. He won.

Would a reasonably minded person who knew the claimant connect the defamatory statement with them? You cannot defame a class of persons i.e. all lawyers are rogues who fleece the public. All priests are immoral and dishonest.

Publication makes known in writing or orally to some person other than the claimant.

Repetition and dissemination this is a fresh publication.

Defences Justification, fair comment, privilege, apology, and offers of amends.

Fair comment has to be on a matter of public interest.

Privilege

Absolute privilege
Statements made in parliament, reports ordered to be published by parliament, judicial proceedings, and matters of state, communications between solicitor and client.

Qualified privilege.

Legal or moral duty, private interests, statements to authorities i.e. complaints, reports of parliamentary proceedings, reports of judicial proceedings, reports of public proceedings.

Limitations of actions.
Limitation Act 1980 torts must be brought within six years. It starts when it would be reasonable to discover the action.

Personal injury within three years.

5

YOU AND YOUR NEIGHBOURS
The Neighbour Principle

We have many neighbours in law. Normally our neighbour is any person who we would reasonably have in mind when we act so carelessly as to cause him or her harm. On this occasion we are talking about our actual neighbours, that is people who live next door to us.

Reasonableness
Fine lines have to be drawn between what is reasonable.

Problems with peace and quiet

Noise as a form of pollution
In all disputes with neighbour, resorting to law should be your last course of action:

- talk to your neighbours
- contact other neighbours
- keep written records
- contact the landlords
- seek mediation

Legal attempts to combat noise
- the police – the police will only intervene if there is likely to be a criminal offence
- local authority – the environmental health department will come round to investigate. The environmental health officer might write an informal letter to the noisy neighbour, this usually will suffice. However, if the problem persists then the local authority can serve a notice under section 8 of the Environmental Protection Act 1990, that is that the noise levels are to be

reduced or curtailed. If the neighbour persists and ignores the notice, the local authority can prosecute.

Going to the magistrates
You can go to the magistrate's court under 82 of the Environmental Protection Act 1990. You have to give your neighbour formal, written notice of your intention to take out proceedings. After that you need to make an appointment with the court and produce your evidence to them. If the court is satisfied, the court will issue a summons against your neighbour.

Going to the county court
This is to start a civil action for an injunction to stop the noise. You can sue for damages once you establish you have suffered damage to your health. Recently the seller of a house failed to inform the buyers that she had suffered from noisy neighbours and had made complaints about them to local authorities. As a result she had to pay the buyer's £15,000 in damages which represented their loss on the house when they tried to sell it some years later.

Increased powers to combat noise
The Noise Act 1996 sets out a permitted level of noise during night hours, that is between 11pm and 7am. The local authority would use an objective standard for measuring noise. If after a warning notice it persists, the equipment can be confiscated and a fixed penalty fine imposed.

Other sources of noise

Noise in the street

Statutory powers to deal with street noise
The Noise and Statutory Nuisance Act 1993 covers nuisance from vehicles, machinery or equipment in the street. It deals in particular with car alarms and burglar alarms.

Car alarms
The person responsible is the registered owner or the driver for the time being of the vehicle. The EHO can serve an abatement notice and then they can:

- immobilise the alarm
- remove the vehicle

The EHO can open and enter the car provided there is no more damage than necessary. The car must also be secured against theft as effectually as when it was found.

House alarms

Householders have to inform their local authority of alarms, which have been installed. The local authority can turn off the alarm by entering the premises, provided he has authority to do so. He can obtain a warrant from a justice of the peace to enter the premises if need be by force. The owner can be called upon to reimburse the local authority for expenses incurred.

Noise from children

There is nothing much you can do with noise from children. There are such things however, as Anti Social Behaviour Orders for children aged ten or over. In 2002 just 466 orders were imposed. They are now becoming more popular

Problems with boundaries and fences

Establishing boundaries

There is no rule of law that requires you to mark the boundary of your property or to enclose it. Community legal funding is not available for boundary disputes. In general, with any conveyance there should be a plan annexed to the register of title or the title deeds.

The objective test

The court will decide what would a reasonable person think he or she was buying at the time and in the circumstances of the case.

When there is no plan

We have to look at the situation in which a plan can be misleading. There are certain legal presumptions; the law makes certain generalisations about boundaries.

Ditches
If there is a man made ditch at the end of your garden that is not marked on any map or plan, then the law assumes the boundary runs up to the near side of the ditch.

Hedges
If there is a hedge at the end of your garden your boundary will incorporate as much of the hedge as you trim. If you trim the whole of the hedge then you may be able to claim that as yours, otherwise the boundary is assumed to be the middle of the hedge.

Hedge and ditch
If there is a hedge and ditch you are presumed to own the land as far as the near end of the ditch, the rule being that you would not normally dig a ditch on someone else's land. If there was a hedge then a ditch, then you are presumed to own the land up to the further edge of the ditch. It is assumed that the ditch digger has thrown the soil on his own land when digging the ditch, and that he has planted the hedge on the bank of soil.

Rights of way
If there is a right of way a boundary is assumed to run in the middle of the right of way, that is the middle of the natural stream of river.

Fences
Where there is no demarcation the general rule is:

- plan with "T" marks – the general rule is where the title deeds have a plan, the usual practise is for there to be a "T" mark on one side of the fence
- no "T" marks at all – it is a general presumption that you own the fence if the supporting posts are on your land
- party fences – you can then decide to have a party fence with both sides owning the fence, and both sides contributing to it's cost of repair

Mending fences
If the fence belongs to your neighbour and it falls into disrepair, he of she is not under an obligation to repair it unless there is some obligation, which has been written in the deeds. If you need to repair a fence at your own expense because it constitutes a danger, you might have to give notice to

your neighbour to go onto his land under the Access to Neighbouring Land Act.

Party walls
The Party Wall Act 1996 provision applies to a party fence/wall such as a brick built garden wall that is astride the boundary between the lands of different owners and separates their properties. There are definitions of what is a party wall.

Liability of owners for third party contractors
Where there is damage of an adjoining building as a result of negligence work to a party wall, the owner may have to bear the responsibility if the builder disappears.

Problems with nuisance
Private nuisance
Private nuisance is defined as something that occurs on someone else's property, which detrimentally affects your property, or your enjoyment of your property. In one case it was held that the ringing of bells in a parish church might constitute a private nuisance, but was not actionable against the Bishop of the Diocese in which the church was situated.

Public nuisance
Public nuisance is something, which detrimentally affects a large group of people and not any individual, usually obstruction of the highway.

Statutory nuisance
Statutory nuisance includes such matters as causing a potential health hazard.

Problems with gardens

Overhanging plants and trees
A general rule is you are entitled to your own space. The branches from neighbouring trees or shrubs, which overhang your garden, are intrusions; therefore they can be regarded as trespass and a nuisance. You are entitled to lop of the branches, which actually intrude over to your side of the fence. You must take great care that only those branches and no others are pruned. You are supposed to return the branch to your neighbour and you are not entitled to keep any apples.

Roots growing underground
Trespass and nuisance can be caused by roots growing underground and into and under a neighbouring property.

Interference with sunlight
You are not entitled to ask your neighbour to cut or prune branches or trees to ensure you have uninterrupted sunlight. You are only entitled to reasonable air space above your property; you cannot impose air space on neighbouring property. You can not insist your neighbour prunes his hedge to a certain height, the problems caused by high hedges can not be over stated. Some house owners have reported problems with property insurance – it can be difficult to change insurers, the premiums can be much higher because neighbours hedge. Some insurers refuse to provide cover at all. In one case a householder had paid £2,500 policy excess due to the close proximity of a 30ft high hedge.

Dangerous trees
Your local authority is under statutory duty to ensure that trees do not impose a danger to either persons or to their property.

Problems with rights and properties

Restrictive covenants
In order to protect the amenities of the area, property owners are frequently resorting to imposing restrictions. These are then covenants registered at the Land Registry and will pass with each transfer.

To impose restrictions there must be two properties and there must be negative covenants. You cannot use a restrictive covenant to insist that your purchaser do positive things. This is usually cloaked in such a way as to not allow the fence to go into disrepair, which of course you have to repair the fence.

Enforcing the covenants the "run" with the land
The new owners should be able to enforce restrictive covenants.

Removing covenants

Applications to a Lands Tribunal
It may be that with the passage of time that they become out of date, and they can be modified eventually by making application to the Lands Tribunal, or they could be changed by agreement.

Easements
Rules on easements
Restrictive covenants may be negative, but easements are positive and these include such matters as right to light, right to support.

Trespass on or access to neighbouring land

Access to neighbouring land

Unlawful access
Unless you are invited onto land, or are there on business, you are a trespasser.

Lawful access
An Act was introduced to get round this problem of householder/trespasser and we now have the Access to Neighbouring Land Act 1992, and gives a temporary right of access, by court order, onto a neighbouring property to carry out reasonably necessary operations, which must be basic preservation work. It does not cover alterations or improvements for their own sake, but covers maintenance, repair and renewal.

Acquiring title to someone else's land – adverse possession
This arises after 12 years without interruption and without permission from the owner who has failed to assert his rights on the property. The Land Registration Act has changed this and the squatter will be able to become registered as owner after 10 years adverse possession. There is however, better protection for registered land against adverse possession, that is squatters, under the new act. The case arise because squatters obtained two free homes worth a total of £300,000 from a local authority in London after the council lost its' attempt in court to reclaim both properties. The High Court held that the council had failed to exercise its' ownership rights over 16 years, and the squatters had treated the properties as their own.

6

YOU AND YOUR JOB
Employment Law

Employment is governed by the law of contract and statute. The original rules derive from common law and still apply today. There maybe two sets of rules applying to the same vent such as an injury at work will be both a civil and criminal matter. Civil under rules of negligence and criminal as a breach of the Health and Safety at Work Act 1974.

Employment

The Contract and its formation
The standard rules apply that is offer, acceptance and consideration.
   Once decided on they cannot be changed unilaterally by the employer
   All contracts of employment like other contracts comprise express and implied terms.

Express Terms
These include information about weekly wages or monthly salary, holidays and sick pay.
   The contract is enforceable as an oral agreement it is a statutory requirement that the employer provides the employee with written particulars of certain terms within two months of the employee starting works section 1 Employment Rights act 1996.
   This does not have to be a formal document in can be contained in a letter. Once a written statement has been issued an employment tribunal will only consider the contents of the statement and not what may or may not have been orally agreed between the parties.

England v British telecommunications plc (EAT) (1990).
An employee complained she had not been given a written contact and when she received one, it was less favourable. She lost as the trial held it was not appropriate for them to remake a contract and the information complied with the legislation.

A newly appointed employee should therefore seek to agree in writing all contractual detail at the earliest date

Remuneration
This is the consideration given by the employee in return for payment to undertake all the duties agree in the contract.

The employees consent must be obtained to make any deductions from wages.

Minimum wage
National Minimum Wage Act 1998 set a national minimum wage of £3.60 per hour for all workers. It is reviewed annually. A sub post mistress only being paid £2.22 was deemed to be an employee the Post Office said she was an agent. A trainee barrister (pupil) was held to be an employee and entitled to the minimum wage.

Working Time Regulations
- Entitled to a break (not defined) when an employee's working day is longer than six hours.
- A minimum of 11 consecutive hours rest on a daily basis
- A minimum of 24 hours uninterrupted rest every week as well as the 11 hour daily rest period.
- The right to be required to work more than 48 hours a week.
- A minimum of four weeks paid annual leave
- Night work must not exceed eight hours in a 24-hour period.

Implied Terms
These apply regardless of what the parties may or may not have agreed.

- Both parties must co-operate in the performance of their responsibilities
- Obey all reasonable instructions. Work done in the past becomes an accepted part of their duties.
- Both parties must take reasonable care performing the contract

Walker v Northumberland CC (QBD) 1994:
The plaintiff suffered two serious breakdowns the employer should have foreseen the risk in the workload. The defendants were in breach of their duty by failing to provide the back up requested,

Employers who do not have a stress policy may be fined under the HASAWA.

An Employee must work in a safe manner.

For example an employee told off for removing a safety guard was in breach of contract and his employer is entitled to dismiss him

An employer's duty of care does not extend to answering questions about a former employee's work record. An employer is under a duty to take reasonable care and will be liable in negligence if it is inaccurate.

An employee must not make use of confidential information or compete against an employer.

There is no overriding duty of an employee to inform his employer of activities being undertaken outside his work

Contracts of employment often contain what are known as restrictive clauses.

The employer must show that such a clause is reasonable. Fitch v Dawes (1921) a managing clerk was prevented form establishing a legal practice within seven miles of the centre of Tamworth the town where he worked and this was enforceable. The restriction lasted a lifetime as the court took the view that clients were lifetime clients.

The court of appeal stated that the courts would not normally grant an injunction where to do so would have the effect of compelling the employee to continue working for his previous employer.

An employer must not break the trust and confidence the employee.

For example carrying out an unlawful business as in **Bank of Credit and Commerce v Ali (1999)**

Unfair or wrongful Dismissal.
This deals with the rights of the employee not to be unfairly or wrongfully dismissed.

Unfair Dismissal

Qualifying Period
This is now one year. Part time-workers (prevention of less favourable treatment) regulations 2000.

They are not to be treated less favourably than those employed full time.

Wrongful Dismissal

Employees who do not qualify may nevertheless bring an action for wrongful dismissal. **Dietman v Brent London Borough council (CA) (1988)**. A child died as a result of injuries inflicted by the mother's cohabitee. In the subsequent report the social worker was found to be grossly negligent and was dismissed.

Plaintiff claimed damages for wrongful dismissal as the Council summarily dismissed her. The court found in her favour because no disciplinary hearing and the report hearing did not equate to gross misconduct referred to in the contract of employment

Employees who have been wrongfully dismissed have to mitigate their loss. He was dismissed and found a job immediately. He was only entitled to the time he was unemployed.

Unfair Dismissal

- Has the complaint been lodged in time
- How was the employees contract terminated

Timing

- 3 months from the effective date of their dismissal.
- when the employer terminated the contract without notice i.e. the employee is dismissed by the employer
- When a fixed term contract is not renewed
- When the employee terminates the contract because of the employer's conduct. This is known as constructive dismissal.

What was the reason given for the dismissal?

An employer must give in writing if so requested one of the reasons listed below or some other substantial reasons.

- *Capability.*
  Physically not able to do the job
- *Capacity.*
  i.e. if an employee gives false information about qualifications.
- *Conduct.*
  Misconduct can take many forms and can range form acts of minor misconduct such as occasional lateness to gross misconduct e.g. assaulting another employee at the work place. An employer must act reasonably when

dismissing an employee on grounds of misconduct. Effect of further evidence of misconduct
No further reasons may be given but further evidence of misconduct may be accepted.

The test of reasonableness.
It must be the same towards all employees. Varied but persistent acts of misconduct eventually add up to gross misconduct.

Redundancy.
Customary arrangement for selection for redundancy
An employee becomes redundant when the job they were doing ceases to exist. Where a customary arrangement exists, an employer must consult with unions prior to dismissal and or employees prior to dismissal on matters such as the exact timing of the redundancies and the employees to be selected for redundancy.

Offer of similar Work
If similar work is available the employer should offer this work to the employee. The employer should make a reasonable effort to contact the employee if the latter is no longer at the place of work.

Transfer of undertakings
Under the Transfer of Undertakings (Protection of Employment) regulations 1981 employees' rights are protected when an undertaking is transferred from one employer to another. If the transfer involves a substantial and detrimental change in the employee's terms and conditions of employment the employee may terminate his employment and treat himself or herself as being constructively dismissed.

Continuity of employment
An employee's continuity of employment is preserved when he is dismissed and subsequently reinstated or re-employed after for example making a claim in accordance with a dismissals procedures agreement.

Insolvency
An employee of a company, which becomes insolvent, is entitled to recover redundancy payment from the secretary of state for trade and Industry

Strike Action

An employee who goes on unofficial strike may be dismissed. An employee who goes on official strike is protected from dismissal for up to the eight week of the strike.

No compulsion to work

Employees cannot be legally compelled to implement a contract of employment, to do any work or attend at any place of work.

Breach of statutory restriction.

It is unlawful to employ someone if it breaches a statutory requirement.

Not in a union

You cannot discriminate against union members.

Criminal Offences

It is illegal to breach a contract that causes a criminal offence i.e. danger to life, valuable property. It is illegal to intimidate another persons to prevent them going about their lawful pursuits.

Dismissal for health and safety activities.

This is where an employee refuses to work in a place he or she reasonably believes to be dangerous.

Dismissal – Procedure

Employers must act reasonably and consistently when dismissing an employee. There must be a disciplinary procedure. Firms with less than 20 employees are exempt from providing particulars of disciplinary procedures.

Remedies

There are a number of remedies, which may be awarded.

- Basic award
- Based on number of years. There may be a minimum amount irrespective of the number of years worked this is not to be less than £3,300 but is subject to a contributory fault on the part of the complainant and refusal of an offer of employment which would have reinstated the complainant.

Compensatory Award.
Up to £51,700 and takes into account the amount which had or could have been earned elsewhere during the period in which the contract existed before the unfair dismissal and payments which exceed the amount of statutory redundancy pay.

Re-engagement may be ordered.
Reinstatement again may be ordered.

Unfair dismissal – essentials for a claim.
Must satisfy the qualifying period, establish that there has been a dismissal, lodge the complaint in time and show that the employer has not given a satisfactory reason for dismissal, or acted unreasonably.

Whistle blowing

Rights in relation to maternity.

Pregnancy
It is unfair to dismiss an employee because she is pregnant.

Maternity leave
Maternity leave will not be less than 18 weeks and can be taken when the employee chooses. This may be extended to 26 weeks from 2003. An employee on maternity leave retains the benefits of the terms and conditions of her employment contract and is entitled to return to the same job.

Parental leave
A parent is now entitled to be absent from work for at least three months in order to care for a child, or if expecting to have responsibility for a child. The Employment Bill 2001 makes provision for new rights for paternity and adoption leave and pay. These include two weeks paternity leave and pay following the birth of a child or the placement of a child for adoption. This must be taken in one single period. Adoption leave around the placement of a child for adoption for up to one year and up to 26 weeks paid leave.

Time off for dependants
Employment Relations 1999. Dependants are entitled to take time off during working hours to provide assistance when dependant falls ill, gives birth, is

injured or assaulted. To make arrangements for care in consequence of the death of a dependant.

Discrimination: sex discrimination, equal pay and race discrimination
Unequal treatment of men and women is made unlawful in three areas. That is:

- their sex or marital status
- the amount they are paid
- their race

Race discrimination
Any discrimination on the grounds of race, nationality or ethnic origin is illegal under the Race Relations Act 1976.

Disability Discrimination Act 1995
From December 1996 the Disability Discrimination Act 1995 made it unlawful to discriminate against a person with a disability.

Health and safety at work

The rules of negligence
An employer owes a common law duty of care to all employees and other persons who may be using his premises

Duty to employees
If an employee is injured at work they may be able to claim compensation from their employer.

Vicarious liability
An employer will be liable for negligent acts of an employee committed in the course of employment.

Manslaughter
When employees are killed at work their employer may be successfully prosecuted for manslaughter.

Health and Safety at Work etc Act 1974
The act sought to involve all persons connected with the work environment in safe practice not just employers.

7

YOU AND YOUR FAMILY
Matrimonial/Family Law

Requirements of a valid marriage
An agreement between a man and a woman to get married. It was prior to 1970 to sue for breach of promise to marry. Marriage is a status and cannot be changed by agreement. Only by operation of law.

Rights and duties on marriage
Under common-law each party is entitled to the other's consortium. Each is entitled to live with the other and share all the comforts and responsibilities necessarily arising out of that relationship.

It is no longer possible for a husband to bring an action in tort for the loss of his wife's consortium and the right to consortium cannot be enforced.

R v R (1991)
A husband cannot force his wife to have sexual intercourse against her will.

Restrictions on marriage.
Since 1753 there have been prescribed formalities that a couple must go though before they are validly married. Calling of banns or obtaining a licence. There are restrictions on who may not be married.

The Prohibited degrees.

Consanguinity and affinity.
No valid marriage can take place where the parties are within the prohibited degrees of relationship. Consanguinity is by blood; affinity is solely by marriage.

The development of the modern law.
Formerly a man could not marry his deceased wife's sister. These were gradually abolished in 1960. In 1986 allowed marriages between in laws and step relation where there is no possibility of abuse of authority. You can now marry your mother in law.

The modern Law
There are now three categories:

Consanguinity
A man may not marry his grand mother, mother, daughter, grand daughter nor his sister aunt or niece. Therefore you may marry your great grandparent. These also cover adopted parents and children.

Step relations.
A man may marry his stepdaughter if she is over 21 and she has never lived with him as if she were his daughter.

Daughters in law.
A man may marry his son's ex wife if they are both over 21 and both his wife and his son are dead.

Effects of the law.

The criminal law.
The prohibited degrees must not be confused with the crime of incest.
Age – both parities have to be over 16. If under 18 parental consent is required but lack of it does not affect the validity of the marriage.

Single Status.
A valid marriage cannot take place where either party was married. The crime of bigamy is not committed if the accused can show that he believed that his first marriage was no longer subsisting, The second marriage will still however be invalid.

Gender
A marriage will only be valid if both parties are respectively male and female. The registrar of births will not however allow a birth certificate to be changed

after say a sex change operation. This area of the Law is currently being challenged.

Transsexual
Again the sex change will have no legal effect as far as the law of marriage is concerned.

Corbett V Corbett (1970)
George Jamison changed his name to April Ashley and Arthur Corbett who knew the circumstances married him. The court ruled that a person's gender is fixed at birth and the marriage had no effect.

The European Convention on Human rights
Applications have been made that the law is contrary to Article 12 guaranteeing the right to marry. All applications have been dismissed.

The future
Opinion is moving towards the needs of single sex couples and the Civil Partnerships Bill 2002 provides for a scheme of formal registration of partnerships.

Polygamous Marriages.
A ceremony which anticipated the possibility of either party taking another spouse in the future could not be contracted validly in England but it is possible that such a ceremony would be a permissible form of marriage in another country and it would now create valid marriage in English law even if both parties were domiciled in England and Wales. The party domiciled in England and Wales could not marry a second person no matter what he original ceremony purported to allow.

Void and Voidable Marriages.
It has no legal effect then it is void. i.e. if either party does not have the capacity to marry. Certain formalities must be complied with.
    Inability to consummate might make the marriage voidable.

Invalidity and failure of marriage.

Methods of terminating a marriage.
The necessity for a final decree. A marriage cannot be brought to an end merely by agreement. It is always brought to an end by a court order known as a decree. There has to be a petition there are three types of decrees nullity, divorce and judicial separation.

A decree is important because it allows the court to award financial provision. In particular the courts have the power to redistribute all property owned by the parties to the marriage including the power to transfer the ownership of property form one person to another. This power is not available where the parties are merely separating.

Nullity
There are six grounds under which a marriage is voidable. Incapacity to consummate the marriage, wilful refusal to consummate that marriage, lack of consent, duress mistake, unsoundness of mind, mental illness, venereal disease, pregnancy, there are two bars, time and knowledge.

DIVORCE

The grounds of divorce.

Proving the ground.
Irretrievable breakdown is therefore the sole ground for divorce. This is a fiction because the court shall not hold the marriage to have broken down irretrievable unless one of the five facts is proved. They are adultery, behaviour, and desertion for two years, separation for two years and separation for five years.

Importance of the facts.
The court must be satisfied that one of the facts has been proved

THE DECREE
A Decree Nisi of divorce will be granted once a relevant fact (and irretrievable breakdown) has been proved. After a period of six weeks the divorce can then be made absolute by a simple application by the petitioner.

Adultery
The petitioner must also find it intolerable to live with the respondent.

Behaviour
The court may find that a marriage has broken down irretrievably if the petitioner proves that the respondent has behaved in such a way that the petitioners can no longer reasonably be expected to live with the respondent. Any sort of behaviour can be relevant

Richards V Richards (1984)
The husband had forgotten her birthday and their wedding anniversary and failed to give her a present at Christmas or when their child was born. He compounded this by refusing to take her out and by failing to get rid of their dog. (Which was causing damage around the house)

Whether the petitioner should live with the respondent
Pheasant v Pheasant (1972)
Husband alleged his wife did not give him the spontaneous demonstrations of affection, which his nature demanded. Petition refused.

Desertion
Has to be two years before the petition.

Separation
Must be a physical living apart but can occur in the same house. Husband and wife slept in different rooms and avoided each other the wife continued to cook for both of them. The petition was refused.

Intention
The respondent must have intended the martial relationship to be brought to an end by their separation no desperation if separated by consent.

Two Years separation
If the parties have lived apart for two years and the respondent agrees to the divorce being granted. Consent must be given on a form issued by the court.

Separation for five years.
Parties lived apart for five years whether the respondent consented or not.

Bars to divorce

Short marriages
No petition for divorce may be presented unless the parties have been married for one year. Prior to that it was three years unless exceptional hardship.

Grave Hardship
A petition alleged five years separation could be opposed on the grounds that a divorce would cause the respondent grave financial or other hardship, and it would in all the circumstances be wrong to dissolve the marriage. Financial hardship can normally be resolved by ancillary proceedings. Only five per cent of all divorces are on the basis of five years separation and therefore this provision is of little practical relevance except in the specific financial circumstances.

General financial protection.
Garcia v Garcia (1992)
The wife's application for the decree absolute to be postponed was granted because of the husband substantial maintenance arrears under a separation agreement registered in Spain.

Children.
A statement of arrangement of children will need to be completed at the time of the petition.

Divorce law and procedure
A divorce may now be granted under a special procedure, which does not require the petitioner to attend court. Over 99 per cent of divorces are undefended. As a result very few couples are now bothered to wait until two years separation has expired as divorce can be obtained much more quickly by one of their alleged adultery behaviour. Over 75 per cent of all divorces are now granted on one of those facts. Most of the law of divorce is now meaningless as divorce can be obtained by consent if the parties are willing to bend the truth or exaggerate slightly. The unnecessary retention of a fault provision can encourage feelings of bitterness and produce antagonism between the parties.

Divorce reform
The idea is that fault is no longer appropriate and the only way would be for one party to file a formal request for divorce with the court. The divorce be

granted after a fixed length of time, unless the court thought that important ancillary matters such as financial or arrangements for the children needed to be resolved. The parties are encouraged to agree ancillary matters in a constructive atmosphere. The act has been passed but the divorce provisions were to be brought into force at a later date.

The family law act 1996 Divorce provisions.
The pilot projects did not go well

Mediation
Mediation is a method of enabling parties to reach agreement on disputed matters without having recourse to court proceedings.

Judicial separation
Grounds for decree – the effects are that the court will have the same powers of ancillary relief.

Financial provision after a final decree

The statutory background.
Under the Matrimonial Causes Act 1973, s. 23; the court has wide powers to grant financial provision on or after a decree of divorce nullity or judicial separation. The courts powers are unlimited. The prime concern of the contract is that both spouses have somewhere to live and in particular that the children will have a settled home. There are several factors that are set out in the act which a court must take not account. Negotiations and agreement between the parties' legal advisors resolve the majority of cases, their final agreement being embodied in a consent order.

Who can apply?
Either party can apply

Orders available to the court.
Maintenance pending suit. Periodical payments to cover the immediate needs of a spouse.

Periodical payments
The basic order. If there is insufficient income at the moment if will make a £1 order, which can be revived later.

Secured periodical payments
It can be enforced by deductions from wages or a charge on the house.

Duration of periodical payments order.
The death of either party will bring the order to an end. The remarriage of the person to whom the payments are made will also terminate the order automatically. Unmarried cohabitation will not bring an order to an end; it may elicit a reduction of the order to a nominal figure.

Lump sum orders.

A specified lump sum.
Transfer of property orders. This can be any property such as shares, household goods, a car, and even the family pets. Usually the matrimonial home.

Settlement of property
Property placed in trust for wife or child of the family.

Sale of property
Typical property orders.

Mesher v Mesher (198)
The court decided the house not to be sold until the child of the marriage reached the age of 17 years.

Martin V Martin (1978)
The court decided that the house would be settled on trust for the wife for her life or until she remarried or ceased to live there.

Pensions

Pensions as capital.
The pension fund therefore represents the couple's joint savings just as much as a joint bank account or the matrimonial home

The basic position
The court has to take into account the pension fund.

Special orders
Earmarking of part of the pension, this will prevent a clean break and will leave the woman dependent on the man's decision when to retire, can now order as splitting of the pension.

Statutory Guidelines
Nowadays the most common form of agreement is the clean break. This creates a clean break financially between the parties. This normally occurs whereby the wife receives a large share of the assets and in exchange she gives up her right to maintenance. This does not apply to the children who are always the responsibility of the parents whilst they are in full time education. The Court will take into account various considerations as set out in Section 25 of the Matrimonial Causes Act 1973.

These include such matters as income, property, the spouse's financial needs, the standard of living, age and length of the marriage, any physical or mental disabilities, the contribution each party has made to the family and benefits such as pensions.

Will Conduct Effect the Financial Outcome
The Courts will only take into account any bad behaviour if it would be unfair not to do so, but generally it is not a factor to be taken in to account in the financial comments.

The Welfare of the Children
The Courts overriding concern will be for the welfare of the children and in such circumstances the Court may allow the wife to remain living in the matrimonial home as she will be looking after the children.

Their maintenance and welfare takes precedence over either of the parties to the divorce.

Even if the wife remarries the former husband will still be liable to pay maintenance for his children.

Consent Orders
Is the case where the parties agree a satisfactory arrangement and these are incorporated into the legal document known as the Consent Order. The

Consent Order contains such matters as the clean break as the only way that the clean break can be achieved is via the Consent Order. Once the Consent Order has been approved and sealed by the Court it is a legally enforceable document.

Splitting of the Assets
Up until the landmark Case of White versus White it was generally thought that the parties usually the wife would receive what was reasonable for her in the circumstances.

It is now seen that there is no reason why there should not be a fifty fifty split of the assets particularly where the parties are wealthy and they may have built up assets during a long marriage. The old rule used to be either one third or one half, nowadays the Courts go towards a more equitable split of the assets.

8

YOU AND YOUR LEISURE
Consumer Law

Goods and Services
Whenever you enter into an arrangement to obtain goods or services you are entering into a contract.

It is not necessary for the contract to be in writing for it to exist. The most common response I receive is, I can't go to court because the contract is not in writing. Very few contracts are in writing. Legally only contracts in relation to the sale and purchase have to be in writing and maybe a contract of employment but apart form that you can go through you life without having any contracts in writing but you are creating and performing contracts all day and every day.

A contract may exist with no words such as when you get on a bus. You have entered into a contract as all the conditions are set out in the company's conditions usually on the back of the ticket or referred to on the ticket.

A contract contains mutual reciprocal rights and obligations both parties must both give and receive something.

Written Contracts
If there is a written contract it may define your legal position whether you read it or not. Terms and conditions a ticket or a receipt can be part of the contract and define your position under it even if you have not signed it. The terms must be reasonable and not unfair.

Signing a contract.
Read something before signing it takes it away to study. Once signed you are bound.

If may contain a clause that the supplier is not liable for any misrepresentation

The clause may be regarded as unfair and therefore unenforceable.

Unwritten contracts.
There is no legal requirement that contracts need be in writing they are enforceable in law whether they are oral or in writing.

Being bound by terms.
You will be bounded by terms you have not read and the court may regard it as unfair if you have no real opportunity of reading the terms.

Usually only parties to the contract can rely on its terms if has been changed so that third parties i.e. recipients of gifts will be able to apply.

Non contractual arrangements.
Terms.
You will be bound by terms you have not read and the court may regard it as unfair if you have no real opportunity of reading the terms.

Usually only parties to the contract can rely on its terms if has been changed so that third parties i.e. recipients of gifts will be able to apply.

Non contractual arrangements.

If you are doing a favour for someone without payment then you are not liable for any default. A contract has to have consideration.

Consumer Protection
There is freedom of contract in English law but you cannot negotiation say an insurance contract and the law has intervened to correct the balance in favour of consumers in certain significant ways.

There may be imposed criminal sanctions for wrongful trading and trading standards officers enforce these laws and prosecute traders committing offences. Their website www.tradingstandards.gov.uk if it is a food question that should go to your Environmental Health Officer.

Implied terms
All contracts include certain terms even though not specifically mentioned and that is such that all goods should be fit for their purpose and of merchantable quality as in a sale of goods contract the law will always imply a term that the goods which are sold will match a sample provided by the seller.

Certain terms automatically excluded from all contracts for example under the Unfair Contract Terms Act a business is not allowed by law to exclude its liability for causing death or personal injury.

Criminal sanctions
Breaches of various codes give rise to criminal liability rather than for compensation claims.

European Law.
It imposes uniform liability for dangerous products.
Unfair terms – the small print regulations.
Business can no longer rely on unfair terms in their contracts with consumers. They must be written in plain and intelligible language. The director general of fair-trading can take action to prevent businesses putting terms in, which are unfair to customers.

It usually persuades firms not to enforce unfair terms

Airlines have been told that non-refundable and non-transferable tickets are unenforceable.

Stop now – The office of fair-trading can issue a Stop Now notice. The regulations cover doorstep selling, timeshare, consumer credit, distance selling, package travel, misleading and comparative advertising.

Discrimination
It is unlawful for a supplier of good to discriminate e.g. refusal of entry to a restaurant for a blind person with a dog. It can affect accommodation, access to public places, baking insurance.

Disability Discrimination Act.
Such as a disabled driver paying more insurance for his car Service providers have to deal with disabled people.

Sale of Goods
Rights are set out in the Sale of Goods Act. The act does not apply to a private seller that is someone not in business.

Obligations of the seller.
These are in every contact.

Satisfactory quality and fitness for purpose.
Goods must be of satisfactory quality and they must be fit for their normal purpose. If say you ask for a microwave with a browning function and you receive a basic microwave then it is of satisfactory quality but not right for the purpose.

If say it is dented, it may not be a satisfactory quality. This is met if a reasonable person taking into account the finish, safety, price, durability and the absence of minor defects as well as fitness for the usual purpose for which the goods are being bought, would regard them as satisfactory.

It is a criminal offence to sell a car in an unroadworthy condition. A shop cannot use an exemption clause such as no refunds or returns if it is not of satisfactory quality.

Extended Warranty
You already have statutory rights and if a defect becomes apparent later you are entitled to compensation for up to six years after the purchase, but you must show the defect existed when you bought the goods and it was reasonable for goods to last that long. The OFT is investigating these types of warranties.

Goods must meet description
The goods must also be as described. Food producers have been prosecuted under the trade descriptions act for describing a product as tender chopped chicken breasts and pure gourds beefburgers, where they were composed of reformed meat and soya.

Seller must give title to the goods.
There is an implied term that the seller has the right to sell. If you buy golf clubs at a car boot sale, which subsequently turn out to be stolen, you have a right against the seller. If you can trace them.

Seller must deliver on time.
They must be delivered within a reasonable time.

Seller must display the price. The retail price must be visible to consumer so that they can the price of products without having to ask.

Guarantees
There is no obligation on the seller or manufacturer to offer guarantees, but if they are offered at no extra cost to the buyer they are legally binding. It must be written in plain English.

Obligation to the buyer
The buyer is obliged to pay the agree price and to take the goods. You cannot change your mind.

YOU AND YOUR LEISURE

Paying in advance by credit card.
You would be protected if you paid by credit card; you can claim a refund from the credit card company. This applies if the price was between £100 and £330,000.

Buyers remedies.
Your remedy is against the shop not the manufacture.

Getting a refund.
If the goods are totally unusable or unsatisfactory from the start, a customer is entitled to a full refund.

Rejecting the goods.
You may have accepted faulty goods and you will then lose the right to a full refund. You need to have a reasonable time to inspect them. If you keep the goods for a considerable length of time you will be taken to have accepted them.
Even after repairs you may still reject them
It is the seller's responsibility to repossess. You should tell them in writing.

Manufacturer's guarantee.
The existence of such a guarantee does not reduce your rights against the shop with whom you actually dealt.

Other ways of acquiring goods
Mail order/E-Commerce
There are various codes effecting this. Traders will have to comply with the Consumer Protection (Distance Selling) Regulations and the Electronic Commerce Regulations 2002. Businesses must provide certain information to include name of the business, contact details, indication of prices, delivery and tax charges.

Sales
Even if you purchase goods in a sale you have the same rights under the Sale of Goods Act. Any notice to the effect that no refunds are made on sale goods is not enforceable in Law. The only proviso might be that the goods might be described as seconds and the Contract is concluded on that basis.

9

YOU AND YOUR LITIGATION
Small claims court and Alternative dispute resolution

If the company or trader you are dealing with fails to answer your letter or refuses to sort out your problem don't be discouraged from pursuing your claim further. Most traders are members of trade associations, which have codes of conduct. Although there is no guarantee that members will follow the code in question if they do not the only effect his may have is that they are expelled form the association.

Many associations offer a conciliation service to help resolve disagreements between consumers and members companies and others can offer arbitration schemes to sort out disputes.

There is now a wide range of ombudsman schemes in the UK. They are completely free and aim to be less complex and time consuming than legal proceedings in many cases upholding the spirit and not just the letter of the law

Going to court is nearly always an option but should be considered only as a last resort. The courts are under a duty to encourage parties with a dispute to consider methods of alternative dispute resolution and to try to resolve their differences out of court. Court action can be lengthy and costly and legal aid is available too only to a few. The small claims track, which is an informal and simplified process, provides and comparatively quick and low cost way of using the courts.

Small claims are dealt with as part of the county court; your local one will be listed in the telephone directory.

Trade associations and codes of practice

First check whether the company you are dealing with is a member of a trade association as the trade association may operate a code of practice to which the member should adhere. If is had breached terms of the code inform the trade association which may be able to persuade the trader to company and, in this case adhere to proper selling methods. It cannot force them to do so. If say you are being harassed by a salesman contact the Trading Standards department who may refer the conduct to the Office of Fair Trading (OFT) as it has powers to take action against traders who use unfair practices and you could also ask the police to intervene

Conciliation
The trade associations to which the trader belongs which will try to bring you and the trader together to reach a mutually acceptable compromise usually offer this. Conciliation is free and informal and may result in the settlement of the dispute. It is often the prerequisite to arbitration in that many trade associations insist on the use of conciliator facilities before the dispute can be referred to their arbitration schemes. It is not legally binding and the trade association cannot force its members to reach a compromise. If conciliation does not resolve the dispute you will still be able go to court or refer the dispute to arbitration. In many industries low cost arbitration schemes are available for, if not you can still agree with the other party use an arbitrator.

Membership of a trade association will not necessarily guarantee you better work or fewer problems. It may offer you some safeguards. ABTA for instance allow the arbitrator to take the requirements of the code into account when deciding the case and there may be a guarantee scheme which pays for work to be corrected or completed if the original contractor goes out of business.

You have a choice as to whether you have the dispute settled by a court or an arbitration scheme.

You can be forced to go to arbitration. The Arbitration Act 1996

Arbitrator schemes are offered as alternatives to court not in addition so you have to choose.

Arbitration schemes generally use written evidence only, so you cannot present your case in person, and it's not always easy to put your case clearly in writing. Court gives you the chance to put your side of the case.

Once you have made your choice the decision of the judge or arbitrator is binding so you cannot have the case re-heard using the other option if you are unhappy with the decisions.

Personal injury

What to do after an accident

- take names and addresses of witnesses. If it's a traffic accident call the police if anyone is injured
- ask you doctor or hospital casualty department to examine your injuries and keep a detailed record
- take measurements, photographs of the scene of the accident, physical injuries or property damage as soon as possible
- write out a full narrative recording the date, the time and the weather conditions if relevant, including a sketch plan where appropriate
- inform your insurers if you think you may be covered for this type of accident
- make a note of details of torn clothing, broken glasses, taxi rides, medical expenses, as these can be claimed as special expenses
- make enquiries to see if similar actions have happened at the same spite

Personal injury claims

Personal injury claims for up to £1,000 can be pursued in the Small Claims Court.
Other claims are usually conducted on a conditional fee basis as community and legal funding would not now be available. There are exceptions to the injury claims not being legally aided, such as criminal negligence, a case involving a new point of law, wrongdoing by a public authority i.e. priests, arising out of a housing claim.

Conditional fees

This is the "no win no fee" arrangement. Solicitors will not charge fees if the case does not succeed. However, because you will still be liable for fees incurred by the other party to the action, great care has to be exercised in pursuing such an option. The ground rule for the no win, no fee scheme are:

- the person who succeeds in the action can recoup the costs of the solicitor's additional charges, the uplift from the other side, including insurance he or she may have taken out to cover the costs if he or she loses.
- defendants can take out insurance against the possibility of losing the action provided they can persuade both the solicitor and the insurer that their case for defence will stand up in court

When can you sue
There is a test of reasonableness. This includes reasonably foreseeable that the harm would result from a failure to take care. There was a duty of cared owed, the duty had not been discharged and damage or injury resulted.

A defendant may have a defence of Act of God, or the plaintiff should have taken reasonable precautions such as walking on an old harbour wall and slipping on a patch of algae and falling. The visitor should have assessed the obvious danger of slippery algae covered stones.

Time limits
In cases of personal injuries or death caused by negligence there is a three year time limit, which runs from the date of injury or the date when the victim knew of this, which ever is the later.

Civil and criminal
The aim of civil proceedings is to compensate the victim, in criminal proceedings it is to fix blame and allocate punishment. Although now in criminal proceedings, courts do have the right to force the accused to pay compensation.

Alternative sources of compensation
Mainly insurance policies, life policies, accident policies, health policies, household and all risk policies, and of course motor insurance.

Alternative sources of compensation
Mainly insurance policies, life policies, accident policies, health policies, household and all risk policies, and of course motor insurance.

Defences to a claim of negligence
The most common ones are contributory negligence. That is:

- where the victim contributes to the accident
- voluntary assumption of risk
- unavoidable accident

The victim may take the risk say if he is taking a lift from a driver knowing he is probably too drunk to drive, or knowing that he is uninsured.

An unavoidable accident might be one, which took place because of a driver's sudden heart attack.

Occupier's liability

The vast majority of accidents happen in the home
Who is the occupier
The fundamental rule is who is in control of the premises. They must exercise a reasonable degree of care to ensure that their premises are reasonably safe for others to use. For example, local authorities responsible for schools, libraries and streets. Shopkeepers, hoteliers and publicans are responsible for their business premises. You are responsible toward any body you invite into your house such as a guest, someone to do a job or for some other lawful purpose such as reading the meters. Your responsibility also extends to others you do not invite, such as authorised ramblers, children tempted by some attraction, trespassers, and undesirables. Your liability towards trespassers has been described as humanitarian only, in other words, you cannot allow a real danger to exist on your property, without taking certain steps to indicate the situation. For example if you have a vicious dog you should give warning notices.

Anyone roaming on your land will not be your responsibility for such matters as natural features, plants, shrubs, trees etc. If there was say an abandoned mine shaft you need to put up notices and surround it with a fence.

Problems with children
Children are tempted to trespass on your property. For example, a small boat was left on council land, boys got into the boat, jacked it up and one was badly injured. The council was liable because they knew of the risk and that the boat would attract children.

Accidents involving visitors
You are under a duty to ensure your premises are safe, such as uneven garden paths for example. You may be responsible for falls by neighbours, friends, postmen or deliverymen.

Accidents in your rented home
If you rent out a home the landlord is usually responsible for the common parts such as lifts and stairs.

Accidents of private property (private premises)
Health and Safety regulations impose criminal sanctions on employers who put at risk the safety of their employees or members of the public.

YOU AND YOUR LEGAL RIGHTS

Defences to a claim
There may be other defences than reasonable care such as an independent contractor, special risks were taken, and adequate warning was given.

Accidents in the street
If you injure yourself on say a loose paving stone; the local authority may be at fault.

Highways
A highway is a road which you cross and the pavement which you walk on.

Highway authorities
These include county councils, metropolitan borough councils, London boroughs, and district or parish councils for certain roads. The local authority's duty is to repair the highways in its area and maintain them in a reasonable condition. What is reasonable is a matter of degree. A reasonable person using the highway would expect some degree of unevenness in a pavement, to take some heed where he or she walks, and would expect more holes in a road than in a pavement.

Other authorities, who would be liable for accidents such as railway, bus or coach accidents. Ships, aircraft, hovercraft.

Accidents at work
Liability for the safety of the workforce depends on a complex interaction between employers' liability for negligence and a growing number of statutory regulations, which have imposed extra strict duties. For example, small firms have a worse record of accidents than big firms. Retail and service industries are just as accident prone as heavy industry.

Employer's liability insurance
By law employers must take out insurance to cover themselves against employees compensation claims. It is a criminal offence not to do so.

When an accident occurs, in the short term the injured employee is entitled to statutory sick pay of up to 28 weeks whilst still employed, or if out of work, to some form of sickness benefit. If they are still unable to work after six months, a claim made be made for long term invalidity or disablement benefit. These benefits do no dis-entitle an injured person from claiming compensation in the form of damages from the employer.

The sorts of claims are:
industrial illnesses – these are work-related illnesses, which cannot be classed as an accident. There have been some very famous cases recently, usually to do with miners, asbestosis.

Scope of employer's liability
The duty of an employer is to take reasonable care, provide safe arrangements, training and work methods. Safe work premises, suitable materials and equipment, competent staff.

Safety legislation
The negligence liability is heavily overlaid with statutory duties flowing from Acts of Parliament, statutory regulations and increasingly, EU directives. The Health and Safety at Work Act 1974 imposes a general duty on employers to ensure, as far is reasonably practical, the health, safety and welfare at work of all employees.

Contributory negligence
Employees have a duty to co-operate with the employer to take care for their own and others safety. Employees who put their colleagues or members of the public at risk be carelessness or by disobeying safety instructions, lay themselves open not only to a claim for damages but also of course, to disciplinary charges and dismissal. Criminal charges are also a possibility.

Staff at risk from the public
New concern for employers as such as in the Suzy Lamplugh case, employers can be held liable if they fail to take all reasonable steps to prevent and guard against the likelihood of risk to their employees. They are under a duty to carry out appropriate risk assessments and brief their staff accordingly.

Accidents involving children
The law recognises that children are vulnerable and unpredictable and what is an obvious danger to any adult maybe an allurement to a child.

When a child causes an accident

Parents liability
Parents are personally negligent in not properly controlling their children. The fault is then theirs in failing to prevent an accident. In the case of a young child accompanied by an adult, it could be that the adult would be hold wholly or partly responsible, i.e. running out in the road.

Children at school
Matters such as safety of premises and equipment, security, negligent supervision are all-important.

Medical accidents
Again doctors and dentists must exercise a reasonable degree of skill so as not to cause foreseeable injury to their patient. Negligence claims are eating up an increasing amount of the NHS budget. as much as four billion pounds, that is 6% of the annual budget. The difficulties of proving negligence are the standard of care required, establishing cause and effect.

The defences to negligence would be medical knowledge at the time of an accident, adequate information provided. The doctor's negligence may consist of failing to provide information to the patient or failing to obtain the patient's consent to treatment.

Other factors are failing to investigate the patient's medical history, failing to provide adequate information for subsequent treatment.

Who is responsible
Under NHS treatment the NHS is responsible.

Emergency services
In a recent case where an ambulance service was slow in responding to a doctor's call so that there was a dangerous delay in getting the patient to hospital, the service had to pay compensation for the resulting deterioration in the patient's condition. On the other hand, claims against the fire brigade, the court held there was no common law duty of care to the public at large to answer a call for help. If therefore they fail to turn up or fail to turn up in time because they have carelessly misunderstood the message, got lost on the way or run into a tree, they are not liable.

Other areas are complementary medicine, veterinary medicine.

Accidents and sport
Public attention, as never before, has been focused on the subject of accidents and sport.

Injuries on the sports field
Failure to observe the rules of sport does not necessarily give rise to liability. There would have to be negligence.

Claiming compensation

General damages

Property damage
When a property is damaged the compensation will be the cost of repairs.

Personal injuries
These include such matters as:

- financial loss
- an amount given to compensate for pain and suffering
- an amount given to compensate for temporary or permanent impairment

Special damages
These cover such things as medical expenses, cost of nursing assistance, cost of disablement aids.

Nervous shock
The damages awarded to victims of an accident will include an amount to compensate for psychological suffering. For example, a policewoman who suffered posttraumatic shock after a colleague unlawfully discharged a pistol in her presence, was entitled to recover damages from the resulting psychiatric injury.

In the case of the Hillsborough disaster, secondary victims, for example relatives of those killed, failed to get damages even though they had seem TV broadcasts of the horrifying events.

Proposals for change
There are anomalies under the current rules. Where a person suffers recognisable psychiatric illness as a result of another persons death, injury or impairment.

For example, a mother was told of a car accident close to her home in which one of her children was killed, another seriously injured. She rushed to the hospital, saw her family within two hours of the accident. She was able to recover damages for the resulting psychiatric illness she suffered. But relatives of the Hillsborough football disaster, some of whom saw it live on TV, went to identify the deceased, where not able to recover damages because they were not close to it.

A father who suffered psychiatric illness on the death of his son three days after the boy was injured in a road accident, was unable to recover damages from the negligent driver. In another case a mother spent three days at her son's bedside, witnessing the tragic end of his life, was able to recover damages for the grief she had to endure.

10

YOU AND YOUR DEATH
Wills, Probate and Intestacy

Wills, Probate and Succession

The distribution of a persons estate depends on whether the person died having made will or intestate that is without making a valid will. The wills have to be in existence at the time of death. Only about a third of the population make a will. If someone dies without a will then the law will deal with the estate under the rules of intestacy.

Like a lot of areas Wills are surrounded by mis-information.

The two most common responses I receive as a solicitor are:

1. It doesn't matter it will all go to the 'wife'
2. Why should I pay your fees, I can get a form from the stationers and make my own Will.

Dealing with the second point, first I understand that barristers, who practice at the Chancery Bar, have a toast, saying 'We toast the man who makes his own Will'.

What they mean is, they make a good living out of 'home made' Wills that go wrong.

This may be a cynical view, and I am sure that a lot of home made Wills succeed to do exactly what the Testator wishes, but at the very least, if you instruct a solicitor to do it and he or she gets it wrong, your beneficiaries will have the opportunity of suing the solicitor, and claiming on his insurance policy if it goes wrong.

Whereas if you are dead your beneficiaries can merely rue the day that you decided to do you own Will.

There are quite specific rules as to how your estate will be distributed in the event of no Will, and it is false to believe that your surviving spouse will inherit their partner's property or that the next of kin automatically acquires the property.

Also any wishes or letters not correctly executed will not be sufficient to be classed as a Will.

It is always better to be safe than sorry, and for the relatively small amount of effort, and cost involved it is better to have a valid professionally drafted and correctly executed Will, than either no Will at all or a home made Will.

Even if you decide to cheat the solicitor of his Will drafting fee, there are many good reasons why a Will should be executed.

It will create certainty as to your Estate, as on an Intestacy, more than one person can claim, become the Administrator, whereas if an Executor/s is appointed, then it is certain as to who has the job and what they are obliged to do.

You also get to choose your personal representatives, whereas on Intestacy the law will decide for you.

In the event of you having children under the age of 18, you can appoint Guardians of your choice. You can also specify what sort of funeral arrangements you require, and ultimately it is a good method to reduce any Inheritance Tax that maybe due.

Wills and codicils

It is a document by which a person sets out his requirements and wishes regarding the administration of the estate that is all his possessions and how it will be distributed.

A will has to comply with the Wills Act 1837. It must be in writing signed by the testator and witnessed by two people. In the absence of this it will not be enforceable.

Codicils

A Codicil is a minor amendment to a Will. The important this about a Codicil for it to be valid is that it should be signed, witnessed and executed in exactly the same way as the original Will.

This is a testamentary document made subsequent to a valid will, which amends or adds to a will. It must comply with the same formal requirements as a will.

Any personal comments or explanations are not prohibited but are more usually contained in a letter placed with a will.

Capacity

Testamentary capacity is that the testator must be over 18 and of sound mind.

There are limited exceptions as to who can make a Will under the age of 18.

The most important being members of the armed forces, who are on active duty or sailor who are at sea at the time they make their Will.

This means that anyone over the age of 14 can make a Will, but obviously soldiers are now only 16 and 17.

Such a person may have made have made a valid Will many years ago, whilst in the Armed forces or at sea, if he has not made another Will since and revoked that previous Will it is still effective.

Animus testandi (an intention of making a will).

It must be made with intention, not under undue influence or fraud. A testator should know and understand the effect of the contents of his will.

The person must have sufficient mental capacity to understand the effects of the Will.

It depends on the severity of the mental illness and they may have, what is known as lucid intervals.

The most important thing is when they sign the Will, if they are capable of understanding the Will will be valid.

If there is any doubt as to the person's mental capacity, then a doctor should be asked whether they believe that person has the capability of understanding the implications of the Will.

This is not a foolproof method, as the Courts may decide that a Will is not valid even if the doctor has given his medical opinion.

Preparing the Will.

Usually a draft will is prepared for approval by the testator. The final print of the will is known as the engrossment and must be signed by the testator in accordance with the formalities required by the Wills Act 1837.

Statutory requirements for a valid will.

It must:

- Be in writing and signed by the testator or by some other person in his presence and by its direction; and
- It appears that the testator intended by his signature to give effect to the will; and

- The signature is made or acknowledged by the testator in the presence of two or more witnesses present at the same time; and
- Each witness either
- Attests and signs the will: or
- acknowledges his signature in the presence of the testator (but not necessarily in the presence of any other witnesses)

In writing and signed by the testator.
This can take any form from a stationer's will, a piece of paper, to one produced by a solicitor. This is known as a holograph will and no particular form of wording is required.

Traditionally the first clauses revoke former wills, appoint executors, dispose of the estate and deal with trustee powers.

Who may sign?
The testator or some other person in his presence and by his direction usually the attestation clause is altered to reflect this.

Signing of the Will
It is very important that the Will is correctly signed, and the date should be put in as the date on which the Will was signed.

It should be put in before the Witnesses sign.

Normally the Will is signed at the foot or at the end of the Will, but this is not a strict legal requirement.

The reason why it was suggested that it should be at the foot or the end, so that nothing further can be added after the Testators signatures.

The attestation clause is merely a statement that the Witnesses were present together and they both saw the Testator sign, and they were present in each other's presence.

Position of the testator's signature
Used to be at the foot or end thereof, now as long as the testator intended his signature to give effect to the will then it will be valid no matter where it is signed.

Meaning of signature
Does not have to be a signed name. Can be a mark, a cross a thumb print or initials have been accepted

If signed by another it must be signed by his direction.
The signature is made or acknowledged by the testator in the presence of two or more witnesses present at the same time.

Acknowledgement of testator's signature.
Testator pointed to his signature saying that is my signature it was then valid. Both witnesses must be there for the acknowledgement and their own signatures.

Acknowledgement of witness's signatures.
If witness signs first they must acknowledge their signatures in the presence of the testator, but necessarily in the presence of each other.

Attestation clause.
Signed by the above named John Jones in our presence and attested by us in the presence of him and of each other.

Competence of witnesses
Witnesses must be competent and they cannot benefit from the Will. If any money is left to the witness, they will not be able to receive it but the Will would be valid.

There is a common misconception that an Executor should not witness the Will. The law has recently changed, so that they can.

Formerly the executor who had an interest in reclaiming costs or with a charging clause could not charge them.

Must not be blind or of unsound mind. Witnesses need not read the will or know the contents.

May a beneficiary be a witness?
A witness or a spouse of a witness will lose their inheritance.

Privileged wills (will of soldiers on actual military service and sailors at sea)
This is one of the exceptions that the Will does not have to be in writing.

S3 enables soldiers on actual military service and seamen at sea to make a valid will even though under 18 any form of words is acceptable so long it is clear from the words that the testator intended them to have testamentary effect.

Example of a will
Main clauses in a will
1. *The revocation of former wills.* The will normally contains an express revocation of any former wills and codicils made by the testator.

I hereby revoke all former testamentary dispositions previously made by me

2. *Appointment of executors.* Usually executors and trustees are appointed

I appoint a of '.......... and B. of .... To be the executors and trustees of this my will.

A testator may will to appoint special executor's i.e. literary executors or a business executor. An executor must have capacity i.e. over 18 and of sound mind.

Funeral arrangements and special wishes concerning the body.
If they are at the beginning they are quickly obvious. There are wishes and are not binding on the executors.

Appointment of guardians
In respect of minor children, married couples have automatic parental responsibility but in unmarried cases the father only has it by court order of by agreement.

Dispositions in the will
These may be a simple gift of money that is pecuniary legacies to specific legacies i.e. items:

- I give free of tax to A the sum of £250
- I give free of tax to B my grandfather clock.

Extension of trustee powers.
Trusts may arise i.e. the beneficiaries might be under 18. The trust arises automatically or a gift for life. The trustees are the people who will look after the estate until someone finally becomes entitled to it in his own right.

The Trustee act 2000 reformed the Trustee act 1925, which will relate to all estates, to provide powers not otherwise given to the trustee.

Powers of maintenance and advancement
Income for the maintenance education and benefit of a minor.

Powers of investment
Power to invest as if they were absolutely entitled. There is however a duty of care.

Powers to purchase or retain a residence.
The authority to retain or purchase a property.
   Powers of insurance
   They have the power to insure trust property.

Powers of appropriation
Trustees are entitled to appropriation i.e. use any assets to meet a legacy without consent of the beneficiaries of the will.

Charging clause
Executors are not paid and only entitled to out of pocket expenses from the estate. Now personal representatives are entitled to receive reasonable remuneration for services provided even if the services are capable of being provided by a layperson.

Powers to carry on a business
He may appoint executors.

Attestation clause
If not included then the probate registry will require an affidavit from one or both of the witnesses confirming that the requirement of the wills act have been complied with.

Gifts contained in a will.

Inheritance tax considerations
It is paid on the estate of a deceased person on the net value of the estate for tax purposes. Currently £275,000 April 04 Thereafter at the rate of 40% on the excess over £275,000
   If testator says nothing then it is free of tax but current thinking is that it is best to stipulate.

I give free of tax the sum of one hundred pounds to my niece Elizabeth Jones.

Categories of gift.

Gifts of land
Real property is land will not strictly involve leasehold since strictly speaking leases are personality.

Leasehold land
Personalty is divided into chattels, that is things real and chattels personal.

I give all my freehold and leasehold property, which I may own at the date of my death free of tax to ....

Failure of gifts of property – ademption
If he no longer had that property it fails.

Legacies or bequest – gifts of personality
Specific gifts not in existence at death will adeeem.

Abatement
If the estate is insolvent then the value of gifts will be reduced to provide for the liabilities.

I give all the rest of my estate both real and personal to ....

The survivorship period.
A gift can be made subject to a survivorship period i.e. it will only pass to the beneficiary provided he or she survives for a specified period usually 21 or 28 days.

Circumstance in which a beneficiary may lose a beneficial interest.

Forfeiture
A person convicted of causing the death of another cannot benefit form his victims death either under the terms of the victim's will, or under the rules of intestacy, see Jeremy Bamber. This may affect his personal representative and

his issue. If manslaughter it will depend on whether he was guilty of deliberate and intentional violent acts.

Beneficiary as attesting witness
The validity of the will is not affected but the witness will lose the beneficial interest.
Any spouse will similarly lose the interest.

Revocation of wills.

Voluntary revocation
A later will revokes a previous will. A codicil may amend or add to the terms of a will and may revoke parts of an earlier will.

Destruction
A will is revoked if the testator destroys it intentionally. It must be done by the testator personally or done on his behalf and in his presence.

Some writing declaring an intention to revoke.
i.e. he doesn't have the original so cannot destroy it. He must write it and sign it like a will.

Revocation by marriage or remarriage
A will is revoked by the testator's marriage unless the will was made in contemplation of the specific marriage, which subsequently occurred.

Revocation by dissolution or annulment of marriage.
Where a testator's marriage is dissolved or annulled after the testator has made a will then it is revoked.

Personal representatives
Appointment of personal representatives. This is the generic terms for both executor and administrators.

Powers and duties of personal representatives.
Executor's duty derives from the will but the administrators derive from the grant of letters of administration.

Obtaining the appropriate grant

They have to establish full and true details of all the assets and liabilities in the estate in order to ascertain the papers which will be required to obtain the grant in respect of the state. A detailed account of the estate has to be given if over a certain limit currently £275,000 even though tax is not payable until £275,000.

The following need to be submitted to the probate registry
- oath – required for all types of grant
- the original will or a copy if the original is not available
- another affidavit which may be required such as the condition of the will
- If any inheritance tax account is required for any reason then a probate summary D18 is required.
- The appropriate fees for Estates
    less than £5,000 – no fee but £1 for each office copy
    over £5,000 – fee of £40 plus £1 for each office copy
- It should be noted that the probate registry now like to see a copy of the death certificate

Collection of assets
Having obtained the grant the personal representatives collect in the assets.

Payment of liabilities
The liabilities are then paid.

Advertisements for creditors.
If a personal representative advertises for creditors then there may be no claim against the personal representatives later.

Distribution
Provided six months have elapsed they since the grant they are protected from claims under the Inheritance (Provisions for Family and dependants) Act 1975

- Check income and capital gains tax. Income and capital gains during the administration period is liable
- Obtain a certificate of discharge of inheritance tax.

Interim distributions may be made
Residuary beneficiaries usually receive a copy of the accounts.

Applying for the grant
It is always under oath. It is sworn statement and will show not exceeding a certain figure.

Inheritance (Provision for family and dependants) act 1975
Must be made within six months of the grant of representation.
  Generally apart from a spouse only someone who is a dependant of the deceased will have valid claim against the estate. Any claim by spouse, cohabitee of or dependent will have to be pursued under the act and the court. The parties can enter into a deed of arrangement that will redistribute the estate.

Inheritance tax

Potential exempt transfers
Any gift made during his lifetime and then survives for seven years the value of that gift does not form part of is estate.
  There is a sliding scale starting after the third year, 80, 60, 40 20 to nil.
  Exempt transfers that is the relief's

- transfers between spouses in life or on death without limit
- gifts up to £3,000 in any one year
- small gifts not exceeding £3,250
- gifts part of normal expenditure which do not reduce the transferees standard of living
- gift in consideration of marriage up to £5000 for parent to a child £2500 where gift is made by party to the marriage y a grandparent or remoter ancestor £1000 by anyone else
- Gifts to charities either in life or on death . . .

Rate of tax 40% after £275,000

Reliefs from tax
Business relief, agricultural relief 100 per cent, farms subject to tenancies 50%

Probate Glossary

Administrator
Someone appointed by the Probate Registry when a Will has not been left

Executor/Executrix
A person named and appointed by the Will to carry out the terms of the Will.

Grant of Probate
The actual document whereby the Executor has received authority to deal with the estate, that is collecting the assets and pay the debts, and then distribute the assets to the beneficiaries.

Intestacy
When someone dies without making a Will

Residuary Estate/Beneficiary
The remainder of the estate after payment of debts and when all other legacies have been distributed.

11

YOU AND YOUR CAR
Motoring

The most likely place you are going to encounter the criminal law is in connection with your car.

Before you go on the road

You must be licensed to drive

It is an offence to drive without a driving licence. They can be obtained from the age of seventeen or over. You must pass a theory and a driving test.

If you are driving with a provisional licence you must drive with a driver who has been qualified for three years and must be over twenty-one, display two "L" plates and inform your insurers, and not drive on a motorway.

A driver is someone in control of a vehicle, which is substantial control. There can be two drivers of a vehicle, say for instance if you were provisionally licensed and the qualified driver gets out, asks you to steer while he pushes the car, then you have committed and offence. You are a learner driver and there is no qualified driver in the car with you.

You can still be in charge of a vehicle when you are not actually driving at the time. If you leave your car on a hill, the car rolls down the hill.

This is very important in cases of drink driving. If you are sitting in the vehicle with the ignition on, you can be convicted of being in charge of the vehicle. Many years ago there was a case of a driver, who had left his vehicle in London, was in a party in Edinburgh. He had his car keys in his pocket and the police took the view that he was drunk in charge of a vehicle. Eventually that case was thrown out, but it does show the lengths to which the police may go.

YOU AND YOUR LEGAL RIGHTS

Renewing your licence when aged 70 or over
As the age of seventy approaches you will be sent a computer-generated reminder. There will need to be a medical declaration, but it is not necessary for a doctor to complete it merely you the driver. Your licence is renewed for three years. This renewal process will be repeated at three-year intervals.

Your car must be licensed too
If a vehicle is kept on a public road there must be a tax disc, unless it is kept on wholly on private land. Therefore if you park on the public highway with no tax disc you are committing an offence. If a tax disc was in force for your vehicle and you do not tax the vehicle because it is not to be used or kept on a private road, you must declare this to the DVLA. This can be done by a Statutory Off-Road Notification. If you fail to make a SORN declaration when you should, you may be fined £1,000.

Number plates
Every car has a unique numberplate.

Distinction between keeper and owner of vehicle
The keeper and owner of a vehicle may not necessarily be the same person. The keeper is the person whose name is on the registration document.

Insuring your car
It is an offence to drive a car, or let others use a car when you are responsible for it, without insurance cover. Insurance is compulsory by law.

Third party
Third party insurance is the minimum cover under the law and will cover damage to other drivers and/or their vehicles if you are involved in an accident for which your driving is responsible. It will also cover passengers in your car. It will not cover damage to your car or personal injury to yourself however.

What you can and can't do when driving your vehicle
There was a high profile case, whereby a woman driver was fined £60.00 for eating an apple at the wheel.
 The question has arisen what can people do whilst driving.
 The law changed recently so it states driver must not use handheld mobile phones or microphones while driving.
 The rules on eating and drinking are a little more vague.

The Highway code states that distractions to be avoided along with loud music, arguing with passengers, reading maps, inserting CD's and re-tuning the radio.

Obviously you must drive with due care and attention and with reasonable consideration for other road users and you must exercise proper control of you vehicle at all times.

It has been agreed that driving one handed whilst eating could be deemed as driving without due care and attention.

Similarly driving at 70 mph along a motorway whilst drinking. Also the Highway Code warns against drivers not operating or adjusting or viewing multimedia satellite navigation or congestion alert systems, if it would distract you attention while you are driving.

Full and frank disclosure
As with other insurance policies you are under a duty to make a full and frank disclosure to your insurers. Full disclosure covers named drivers, previous convictions, and type of use and involvement in an accident.

The Motor Insurers' Bureau (MIB)
The Motor Insurers' Bureau was set up to provide cover against drivers who have caused an accident but have no insurance cover, or who cannot be traced – the hit and run driver. All motor insurance companies must belong to the MIB by law. It pays out compensation, which the court decides should go to the accident victim, who would otherwise be deprived because of the driver's lack of effective insurance.

Vehicle checks
Maintaining your car – offences
It is an offence to drive a car unless the following are in good working order:

- seat belts
- brakes and steering gear
- lights
- windscreen, windscreen wipers and washers
- demisters
- tyres – including spare
- silencer
- exhaust system

The "MOT" Test
If a vehicle has been registered for more than three years, it is an offence to use it on a road without a current test certificate.

In order to drive a vehicle
You will need:

- driving licence
- car insurance
- registration documents
- current tax disc
- MOT certificate (if your car is more than three years old)

Seat belts
It is an offence to be a driver or front seat passenger without wearing a seat belt, unless a special exemption applies. Similarly, rear seat passengers must wear a seat belt if fitted.

Buying a car

Buying a car from a dealer
A dealer is someone who sells in the course of business. You will obtain basic protection under the Sale of Goods Act. A dealer's legal requirements are:

- the car will be fit for it's normal purpose
- it is of merchantable quality
- it conforms to it's description given to you
- he has the right to sell it to you

A private seller is not bound to you under the Sale of Goods Act.

Stolen cars
A vehicle cannot be purchased without the consent of the owner, regardless of the buyer's knowledge of intent. So if you buy a car that is stolen you have no option but to hand the car over to the police. The law favours the true owner.

YOU AND YOUR CAR

Buying privately
The only obligation the private seller has is that any particular specified by him must be true. If you have a complaint against a private seller you will be in difficulties.

Buying at auction
You will have considerably restricted ability to make a claim for legal remedy if the car proves to be defective.

Accidents
You must report an accident to the police when it involves injury to another person, damage to another vehicle or to an animal – but not a cat, property adjoining a street or street furniture which normally means lamppost, bollard etc. You must also stop after an accident.

Obligations to report an accident
You are required to stop and produce your insurance details. If you cannot do it at the time, a report must be made to the police within 24 hours. Insurance details must be produced within 5 days. Again, if there is no one around at the time, you must make a report of the accident within 24 hours.

Insurance certificate and driving licence
It is advisable to keep your insurance certificate in your car at all times, and not to drive without your driving licence. These precautions can reduce the inconvenience of having to attend at a police station to produce either document.

Car theft
Theft – this involves an intention to permanently deprive the owner of his possession.

Taking a vehicle without consent, or "joy-riding"
This is a separate offence from theft, as it is not taken to permanently deprive the owner.

Offences and penalties

Offence

Dangerous driving offences

Meaning of dangerous driving
A person is regarded as driving dangerously if the way he drives falls far below that would be expected of a competent and careful driver.

Careless driving offences
This is by far the most common. Examples of careless driving are:

- crossing a white line
- failing to stop and look at a T-junction
- edging on to a road when the view is obstructed
- reading a map etc in a car

Drink drive offences
The legal limits are:

- 35 micrograms of alcohol per 100 millilitres of breath
- 80 milligrams of alcohol per 100 millilitres of blood
- 107 milligrams of alcohol per 100 millilitres of urine

If you refuse the breath test, or providing a specimen, it is a separate offence.

Random breath testing
You must give the police reasonable cause to suspect you are over the limit. For example, by driving erratically or by committing some motoring offences.

Penalties
A person convicted of a drink driving offence is liable to a maximum term of imprisonment of six months and to a fine of £5,000. Obligatory disqualification of either twelve months is also applicable.

Repeat offenders

The disqualification period may be longer than twelve months. For example a second drink drive offence in the space of ten years will result in a minimum of three years disqualification.

Speeding offences

Maximum speed limit for cars is 70mph. Cars towing caravans and trailers 60mph. Buses and coaches 70mph, these are on motorways. Goods vehicles 70mph – goods vehicles exceeding 7.5 tons 60mph. 30mph limit applies to all traffic on all roads with street lighting in England and Wales unless signs show otherwise.

MOTORING

The legal background to selling a car.

The usual rule for a private sale in Caveat Emptor (let the buyer beware).

An agreed buyer may be able to sue for misrepresentation

If the car in negligently misdescribed, the seller is liable for a false description, even if he believed that description to be true.

The purchaser may also have ground for a breach of contract claim if the seller made a specific statement that proved to be false, such as the car had a new clutch fitted.

General statements such as the car is in good condition are subjective and so are unlikely to form the basis of a claim.

12

YOU AND YOUR BUSINESS

The various forms of business organisation, which person or person may choose to operate a business. Each, which may offer a number of advantages and disadvantages, most common forms, are Sole Trade, Partnership, Private Limited Company, and Public Limited Company.

Sole Trader
1. He or She alone has the sole right to make all decisions affecting the business
2. Owns all the assets to the business.
3. Responsible for paying Income Tax and receives all the Profits on the Business
4. Responsible for Debts and obligations of the business without any limit.

Partnership
Consists of two or more persons who are on the basis of a contract between themselves.

1. Share the right to take part in making decisions, which affect this business or the business assets.
2. Share the ownership of all the assets
3. Share the net profits of the business, although there may not be equal shares.
4. Share responsibility for the debts and obligations of the business without any limit, although if one does not pay, the others must pay his share.

Private Limited Company
The business is run as a Private Limited Company, which will be owned and operated by the Company itself. The Company is recognised in Law as having a personality, which is separate from the person or the persons who formed the Company, and from the Directors and Shareholders.

In many private Companies the same persons hold the positions of Shareholder and Directors, but the distinctions must be observed, since the validity of many decisions may be in question if the appropriate formality has not been observed.

Decisions of Directors
The Directors will be responsible for making the following decisions

- Entering into Contracts
- Other matters of day to day management
- Calling general meetings
- Taking legal proceedings in the Company's name
- Approving the registration of the transfer of shares.

Decisions of Shareholders
The shareholders are responsible for making various decisions, such as altering the aspect of the Company's constitution.

- Dismissing a Director from the Board
- Appointing Directors to the Board
- Condoning any Breach of Duty to the Company by its Directors

Shareholders will also be responsible for authorising the Directors to issue shares, enter into contracts with individual directors, by which the Company will buy from or sell to that Director something of a significant value. Awarding to individual director's service contracts of significant duration.

Decisions of shareholders will normally be made by prescribed percentage, which depends on the decision in question. Some decisions, such as dismissing or appointing directors, require a simple majority, and are ordinary resolutions, some such as altering their Company's name or its regulations are a special majority, being 75% and are described as Special Resolutions.

Assets
The Company may own assets of the business or though it may have been agreed, that it will use an asset, which is owned by one of the Shareholder individually.

Taxation
The Company will pay Corporation Tax on the profits of the business. The directors and Shareholders cannot be made liable for payment of Corporation Tax.

Typically Directors and Shareholders received income from the Company, the form of Salaries and Dividends. Both of which give rise to a possible charge to Income Tax, dependant on the individual.

Debts
The Company is only responsible for the Debt and Obligations of the Business. Shareholders enjoy the benefits of a limited liability, which means that their liability is limited to paying the Company the price they agreed to pay for their shares.

There are only a few exceptional circumstances, such as where the individual has acted dishonestly, where are directors or shareholder can be forced to make a contribution to the Company's assets in the event of insolvency.

Publicity
In return for the Limited Liability, the company has to accept a considerable degree of publicity of information about itself, its Directors, its Shareholder, and its Finances.

Prescribed information is required to be filed with the Registrar of Companies in Cardiff and updated as necessary. All information filed with the Registrar of Companies is open to inspection by the public.

Public Limited Company
To be a Public Company, the Company's constitution must state that it is a Public Company, and must have the words Public Limited Company or PLC at the end of the Company's name

Dealings in shares of a Public Company
A Public Company may apply to have its shares listed on the Stock Exchange or the Alternative Investment market, and this means the price will be quoted on which dealing in the Company shares will take place.

Listed Market
Only a large Public Company, which has traded for a least three years, can apply for its shares to be listed on the Stock Exchange. This means that these are amongst the most marketable of all shares, only around 2000 of the UK's Companies are listed, compared with over a million companies registered in the UK.

The Alternative Investment Market
This was set up in June 1995; it is less stringently regulated

The Companies Act requirements are that a Private Company need not comply with as many regulations as the Public Company. The Private Company need only have one Director and one Shareholder. The Public Company must have a least two Directors' and at least two Shareholders.

The Private Company can buy back the Shares of a member who wishes to leave.

The Private Company is prohibited from offering to issue its shares to the public at large.

Differences in practise in a Private Company, Directors and Shareholders are often substantially the same persons.

Legal and Practical considerations when Starting a Business
Employees
There is A Statutory duty under the Sex Discrimination Act 1975, and the Race Relations Act 1976, not to discriminate, on the grounds of Sex, Race or Marriage status in advertising or offering employment.

Similarly with regards to membership to a Trade Union.

There is a further duty under the Equal Pay Act 1970, with employers to provide equal pay for men and women where employed, to do the same or comparable work.

Statement of Terms and Employment Rights Act 1996.

Section 1. Within two months of commencement of employment, the employer must give the employee a written statement setting out the main points.

- Identity of the Employer and Employee
- Date of Commencement of the Employment
- Date of Commencement of any previous employment, whether the business has changed hands.
- Pay and intervals of pay.
- Hours of Work
- Holidays and whether holiday pay is given
- Arrangement for Sickness and Sick Pay.
- Pensions
- Period of Notice
- If employment is not permanent, the period of which it is expected to continue.

- Job Title
- Place of Work
- Particulars of any collective agreement
- If the employee is required to work outside of the UK
- Disciplinary Rules
- Grievance procedures
- Whether the Employer has obtained a contracted out certificate in connection with State Earning Related Pensions Scheme.

Tax and National Insurance
The Employer is required to operate a PAYE system, thereby deducting from his employee's pay the appropriate amount of Income Tax and National Insurance, and account for these deductions to the Inland Revenue.

Health and Safety
An Employer has a Common Law to make and take reasonable care for the health and safety of its Employees at work, including the provision of:

- Competence of fellow workers
- Safe plant and equipment
- Safe system of work

Certificate of Insurance
The Employer is required to carry insurance against his liability to an Employee who is injured or who contracts a disease as a result of his work.

A Certificate of Insurance must be displayed in the place of work.

Future Dealings with Employees
Other matters to take into account are:

- Time off work for ante Natal Care
- Trade Union duties
- Public Duties

If the employer fails to give the employee the appropriate period of notice of dismissal under the contract, he will have a claim for damages for breach of contract, wrongful dismissal.

An employee, who is made redundant, after two years qualifying service, may be entitled to be paid redundancy payment by his employers.

Accounting Records for Tax Purposes

National Insurance – sole trader or partner will pay Class 2 National Insurance, also Class 4 National Insurance contributions, which are calculated and entered as Taxable profits. A Limited Company will pay the employees National Insurance contributions in relation to each of its employees, including directors and will collect and pay the employees own Class 2 National Insurance contributions.

Value Added Tax

If the annual turnover for the Business is expected to exceed £58,000, this is adjusted annually, in the ensuing thirteen weeks, the proprietor must register for VAT.

Licence and Consumer Credit Act.

If the business involves offering credit or hire facilities, the owner may require a licence under the Consumer Credit Act 1974. This may be obtained from the Office of Fair Trading.

Other Licences

Particular types of business's requires a Licence to operate, these can be obtained from the appropriate local administration offices, such as

- Liquor Sales
- Food Manufacture
- Children's Nursery

Insurance

A range of possible insurance should be considered to which employer's liability and a third party liability are compulsory.

Examples on non-compulsory are Fire, theft, Product Liability and Motor Insurance.

Intellectual Property

The business may be using inventions, design or products, which can be protected from copying by competitors, by registration.

This is a Patent, Trademark etc.

Sole Trader

Taxation of Income and Income profits

A sole Trader may make two types of profit, Income and Capital. If they are recurring by nature, Trading, Rent, Interest, a sole trader will face a possible charge to income tax. If the profit derive from disposal of an asset owned by the sole trader, such a business premises, he will face a possible charge of Capital Gains Tax.

The profits of the business will derive mainly from the carrying on the trade and would therefore be assessed for Income Tax.

Receipts of the Trade less Income Expenditure

The profits of the Trade are the chargeable receipts of the Trade less its' deductible expenditure.

Receipts of the Trade are those, which derive from trading activity other than from circumstances not directly, connected with the Trade. Most receipts of the Trade, such as Sales are easily identified, but some less so, such as the cancellation of a trading contract, as compensation would be a receipt of trade, but a gratuitous sum received on termination of the trading relationship would not be. The former would attract Income Tax, the latter would not.

Receipts of a Trader, are only chargeable to Income Tax, if they are an income as opposed to a Capital nature, therefore an Antique dealer buying stock would result in income, whereas the same item used for a persons office and sold many years later, would be Capital.

If the items recurs such as Gas, Electricity, Telephone charges, Staff salaries, it is of an income nature. Expenditure on the purchase of Fixed Assets would be Capital.

To be wholly deductible the expenditure must be incurred wholly and exclusively for the purpose of the Trade.

There was the famous case of the Barrister, trying to claim for her Black garments, which she said she would never wear outside of Court, and she wasn't allowed to.

Capital Expenditure

This will qualify for Tax relief under a separate system, under the Capital Allowance Act of 1990. This is in respect of machinery and plant, which is not, defines, but plant includes the businessmen for carrying on his business, except stock in Trade use.

Examples of machinery and plant are cars, vans, office equipment, computer software, tools and manufacturing equipment.

The tax payer is allowed each year to have a writing down allowance of up to 25% of the reducing balance of the cost, in calculating his taxable income.

Running a Business in Partnership

Where two or more persons which establish a business relationship between themselves, without becoming a Company, a partnership is only one of a number of possibilities to the employer, principle and agent, franchiser and franchisee.

What is a Partnership

A partnership arises when two or more persons agree that they will run a business together and actually do so. The agreement can be oral or in writing or maybe implied by conduct. A partnership need not necessarily be recognised by the parties since the existence of the partnership depends on whether or not the definition contained in Section 1 of the Partnership 1890 applies. The partnership is a relation who subsists between persons carrying on a business in common with a view of profit.

Fundamental Characteristics

Typical examples of what a Partnership include are:

- Right to be involved in making decisions which affect the business.
- The right to share in profits of the business
- The right to examine the accounts of the business
- The right to insist on openness and honesty from fellow partners
- The right to veto the introduction of a new partner
- The responsibility to share any losses by the business

Setting up a Partnership

There is no necessary formality; it is useful if the partners have a written agreement.

Formalities required by Statute

Business Names Act 1985.

There are controls over the choice of partnership name and requirement to reveal names and addresses of the partners.

The controls and requirements will not apply if the name simply consists of the names of the partners.

Certain words will require the Secretary of State for Trade and Industry prior permission, such as Royal International Etc.

On all stationary all prescribed information must appear. This information consists, of the names, the partners, and an address in Great Britain for service of documents. Non-compliance of the obligation is and offence, punishable by fine and the Partners will be unable to enforce contracts is the other party can show that he was prejudiced by the non-compliance.

Trading Partners cannot have more than twenty partners; professional partnerships are not limited in this way. It is provided therefore the partnership can instead include on its stationary a statement of full list of partners is available at the principal place of business.

Other Statutory Obligations
These include returns for Income Tax, VAT and National Insurance.

APPENDIX

Recent changes in the Law
The law, of course, is in a continuous situation of change. We have enough problems just keeping up with domestic law, let alone edicts from Europe, International Courts, and the Court of Human Rights. Our law now comes from many sources. As we learnt, it is mainly split into Civil and Criminal Law. There are four legal sources of law, namely, Custom, Judicial, Precedent, Legislation and European Law.

Recent Changes
Home Sellers Pack
This government has been insistent on trying to introduce the Home Sellers Pack, whereby the Seller of the property will need to provide a certain amount of information.

It has become bogged down because part of the proposals was that there would be a survey in there, which the Seller would pay for. There was much discussion as to whether anyone would accept a Survey prepared by the Seller. Recently the Law Society have said that the Home Sellers may have to make available a wide range of sensitive information about their homes such a security systems, tot he general public if Home Information Packs become compulsory. The Government plans to introduce the packs into the new Housing Bill now going through Parliament. Any member of the public will be able to insist on getting the pack and the Law Society claim that this could be open to abuse by burglars, stalkers and snoopers

Solicitors Self Regulation
The Law Society is able to regulate solicitors and there is constant political pressure for this self-regulation to disappear. The are always complaints about the way complaints are handled.

Lawyers Lack IT Skills
Lawyers are ignorant when it comes to IT and many are not prepared to put in the effort to understand even simple technical details, a survey of Legal IT professionals revealed. A recent survey was asked what were the worst aspects

of working for Lawyers, they said apart from the ignorance of IT, they said that they included a lack or project management skills, poor commercial awareness and a tendency to approach IT in the same way they deal with their legal work.

Lawyers are trained to find flaws in documents, a trait they carry over into every aspect of their dealings with all projects therefore they don't get the big picture and are overly pedantic.

They find it hard to stop approaching everything as if it were a Contract or Negotiation.

A recent survey also said that on 40% of Lawyers had a PC on their desk.

Public get direct access to the Bar

Members of the public can now instruct a Barrister directly. Barristers can provide their usual services of specialist advice drafting and advocacy to the public without having to instruct a solicitor first. Barristers will not be able to take on a solicitors role in the conduct of litigation now will direct access be permitted in criminal, family or immigration work. They can take instructions from intermediaries such as independent financial advisors seeking tax advice for a client.

Only those Barristers, who have been in practice for three years and having completed a special training course, will be able to take advantage of this scheme. The cab rank rule does not apply and Barristers may not handle Clients money.

Public access to Barristers was allowed until the 1950's, this would suit businesses and individuals that do not need the administrative services of a law firm.

Civil Procedure Reforms lead more disputes to be resolved by pre-action correspondence and there is a growing opportunity for clients to achieve a dispute resolution with the assistance of a Barrister and without the cost of a solicitor.

The Law Society supports this to widen the choice of consumers of Legal Services.

Over the last few years, Solicitor advocates have been chipping away at the Bar's market and there may be a suggestion that there will be fusion, that is, no distinction between, Solicitors and Barristers. Many other jurisdictions have now no distinction, Australia, Canada and America.

Giving the Deceased the last Word

Why shouldn't a video Will be valid, under the current system, video or even tape recordings would not be valid. The law often fails to keep pace with technology and the area of will is no exception. The current legislation dates back to the Will Act 1837, well before the advent of modern communication.

Section 9 states that a will is not valid unless it is in writing and signed by the testator. Australian Law has a similar provision, but there has recently been a general dispensing power for courts to submit documents that do not comply with the requirements of section 7. If they are satisfied that they are intended by the deceased to constitute the will. Michael Edward in 1993 left his estate by way of a will, later he decided to make some specific gifts and made it the subject of a separate list attached to the will, he made the list in tape format, and included a clause in his will directed at his executors to dispose of his will in accordance with it.

The court was satisfied that the deceased made the tape before the execution of the will and has been clearly labelled. The court decided although there was a rambling presentation that the contents were sufficiently certain to dispose of the deceased estate and it was submitted to Probate.

The problem would also arise as to authenticity.

One solution might be to establish a central register, where solicitors could make a record of such will, even if the will is in the care of a solicitor, there is no guarantee, that the departed had not made a later will with another law firm. A registration scheme may overcome these problems and identify that latest will of the deceased. After almost 170 years, maybe it's time to look at the system afresh to ensure its keeping up to date with modern technology.

Strength in numbers

After the Second World War the number of solicitors was about 13,000, the lowest figure since 1880.

Since the 1950's, the profession started to grow, in 1951 there were 17,936 practising solicitors, equating to one for every 2,500 residents in England and Wales. There are now a record 92,752 practising solicitors as at 31st July 2003, a 4.2% rise on the year before, and in line with the annual trend over the last 30 years. That equates to 565 people per solicitor. The competition is getting fiercer.

The trend since the 1970's is growing by 50% every decade using population projections from the Office of National Statistics, this means 418 per solicitor, 2011, 290 in 2021, and 236 by 2026, at that rate there is a lightly scary long term future scenario which every person in the country will have their own exclusive solicitor. Number of women account for 40% of solicitors on the roll, at that rate of increase it will be less than 10 years before women are in the majority, the younger end of the profession 50% practising solicitors aged 30 or younger are women, there is a slow decline in the number of law firms and offices, there were 9,198 firms and 12,708 offices in total including branches representing drops of around 9% since 1997. There are 4,117 sole practitioners, 3668 firms of two or four partner and 911 firms of 5–10 partners, 358 firms of 11–25, 106 firms 26–80 and 38 firms of 81 or more. The last category which makes up 0.4% employs more than 22% of all private practise solicitors. During the period 2003 the number of partner promotions fell because the situation in the market was worse, the number of students applying and being accepted on an under graduate law course dropped.

A third of all trainees work in the 38 firms of 81 or more partners, and male trainees are much more likely, than female trainees to be placed in those firms are.

GLOSSARY

ABSOLUTE TITLE   On registered land this is the best title that is given by the Land Registry.

ABSTRACT OF TITLE   In unregistered conveyancing this is usually photocopies of the seller's title for the last 15 years, now obsolete, as registered land has taken over.

ACKNOWLEDGEMENT OF SERVICE   In litigation process where summons has been issued, the defendant normally has to Acknowledge Service.

ACTUS REUS   An Act which is illegal, such as theft, that is the guilty act.

ACTUAL BODILY HARM   Hurting another person, but less severely than that would amount to grievous bodily harm.

ADVERSE POSSESSION   Intentionally occupying land to prevent the rightful owner or tenant of using it (Squatting).

AFFIDAVIT   This is a sworn statement usually used in court process.

ADJUDICATION   Official declaration that the document is correct.

ADMINISTRATION OF ESTATES (SEE PROBATE)   When no will has been left, the Administrator may administer it.

AGENT   A person who acts on behalf of another and combines his principal. An agent can become as legally liable as the principal and vice versa.

AGGRAVATED ASSAULT   A more serious type of assault, such as one leading to actual bodily harm.

AGGRAVATED BURGULARY   Entering premises armed with a weapon intending to steal goods.

ALIBI   Claim that a person was elsewhere when a crime was committed.

ALTERNATIVE DISPUTE RESOLUTION   These are methods of resolving disputes without having to go to court and the recent court reforms it is recommended that all forms Alternative Dispute Resolution are undertaking before court action is started.

ANCILLARY RELIEF This is an application made to the court in divorce cases, which resolves the situation between property and children.

APPORTIONMENTS When outgoings such as rent, insurance, service charge have been paid either in advance or in arrears, and adjustment has to be made on completion.

ASSAULT When threatened with physical harm may result even if the person threatened is not touched.

ASSURED SHORTHOLD TENANCY A type of tenancy agreement under which the landlord has the right to take the property back at the end of the tenancy agreement.

ASSENT A transfer of the property once probate has been granted.

ASSIGNMENT Transfer of a lease or intangible asset such as insurance policy.

ATTACHMENT OF EARNINGS A court order that deductions may be made from a persons earnings, the employer pays the money the court and the court then pays the money to the people it is owed to.

ATTESTED Either sworn or signed in the presence of an independent witness.

ATTORNEY A person appointed to act for another person as and when they cannot look after their own affairs.

BAIL Either to pay or promise to pay t an amount of money so that an accused person is not put in prison before the trial. Bail money can be lost is they do not appear.

BANKERS DRAFT Cheque drawn by a bank on itself, it is used there must be certainties that a cheque will be paid.

BARRISTER Lawyer usually instructed by solicitors to either give their legal opinion or act as an advocate in court proceedings.

BATTERY Using physical force on someone either intentionally of carelessly without their agreement.

BENEFICIAL OWNER Person owning land, for their own benefit.

BENEFICARY With respect to land, that person has the beneficial ownership and receives rent or is the occupier. Under a Will the person to whom the estate given.

CAPACITIES Parties to a contract must have capacity therefore minors, that is those under the age of eighteen or those of a mental disorder who are not capable of entering into legal contracts.

CARELESS DRIVING Driving a motor vehicle on a road without due care and attention or without reasonable consideration for other persons using the road.

CAUSE OF ACTION The ground of which an action can be maintained but often extended to any claim on which a given action is in fact grounded, whether or not legally maintainable.

CAVEAT Some sort of warning or condition.

CAVEAT EMPTOR Let the Buyer beware.

CAUTION Caution may be registered with the Land Registry, so that the person putting on the caution will be made aware of any transfer or disposition of the land.

CERTIFIED COPY/OFFICE COPY A certified copy may be made by solicitors. A certified is a true copy; an office copy is usually an official copy from either the Land Registry or Probate Registry and can be used in exactly the same way as the original.

CHANCERY DIVISION A section of the High Court that deals with Trusts, Land, Company Law, Patents and so on.

CHARGING CLAUSE – WILL A vital clause whereby professional executors such as solicitors and accountants are entitled to charge.

CHATTEL Any property except Freehold land.

CHATTELS Another expression for fixtures and fittings.

CLERKS OF THE JUSTICES A Solicitor or Barrister who helps in court by advising the magistrates.

CODICIL Extra pages to change a valid Will which needs as minor alteration. The Codicil must be signed and witnessed and then attached to the Will.

CO-OWNERSHIP Either tenants in common or joint tenants.

CONSIDERATION It is absolutely necessary that in any form of legal enforceable contract there is consideration. The consideration does not have to be adequate in merely has to exist, anything else is a bare promise and cannot be legally enforced.

CONTACT ORDERS Whereby the part without residence of the child is able to contact the child either physically or by telephone.

CONDITIONAL FEE AGREEMENTS Also known as 'no win no fee'.

CONTRIBUTORY NEGLIGENCE This may reduce the injured party's damage if he or she has contributed to the accident.

COPYRIGHT Exists without any formal registration or declaration and the copyright owner must give their permission for items of which they own the copyright to be reproduced.

COUNSEL Another name for Barrister.

COUNTERPART Either a signed document or usually a lease, the original is signed by the tenant, the counterpart is signed by the landlord, and exchanged.

COVENANT Legal promise usually contained in a deed.

CONVEYANCE Now obsolete as documents are transferred under the registered process, even if they are still unregistered.

DANGEROUS DRIVING Standard of Driving which falls far below that of a careful competent driver and it would be obvious to such a driver that is was dangerous to drive that way. Such a driver may be disqualified from driving by the Court.

DEATH AND CONTEMPLATION OF One of the exemptions to property being left by a will, can be left by words in contemplation of death.

DECREE ABSOLUTE The final Court order which ends a marriage.

DECREE NISI A provisional court order which orders that a marriage should be dissolved.

GLOSSARY

DEFAULT JUDGEMENT Failing to do something, which has been agreed to be done.

DEVISE Means to leave Land in a Will.

DISCLAIMER To give up a claim or right or refuse to take over an onerous contract. Can also limit responsibility.

DISBURSEMENTS What the lawyers call payment they may out on behalf of clients such as VAT, Land Registry searches, and Registry fees, Stamp Duty, Inheritance Tax payable on an estate currently (£275,000).

DURESS Threatening or pressurising someone to do something.

EASEMENT A right granted by one landowner to the other, such as right of way, right of drainage water etc.

EQUITY Usually described as fairness or the difference between the mortgage and the value of the property.

ESCROW Where a deed is signed and delivered conditionally, upon some of them taking place, such as exchange of contracts or completion.

ESTATE There are two estates in land being Real Property, which is either Freehold of Leasehold, and the Personal estate relates to anything that is not land.

EXCHANGE OF CONTRACTS When contracts are formerly exchanged after which time both parties are bound to proceed.

EXECUTE Formal word for sign.

EXECUTOR The person appointed by the will to carry out the provisions of the will. Probate needs to be granted before the executor can sign or transfer any part of the real or personal estate.

EVIDENCE Evidence given in Court to something said to the witness by another person.

FEE SIMPLE Legal terminology for Freehold, which is Fee Simple absolute in possession.

FILED PLAN The official Land Registry plans.

FIXTURES AND FITTINGS Usually described as the items that can be removed from the property and a separate list is made on the sale of the property.

FREEHOLD The absolute ownership of the land from the centre of the earth to the skies.

FLYING FREEHOLD Part of the property, which may be above an alleyway or corridor or overhanging, another other parts of the property which is owned by somebody else.

GAZUMPING The seller after agreeing the sell but prior to exchange of contracts increasing the price and selling either to another purchaser or the original at the increased price. There are always plans to outlaw this.

INHERITANCE TAX Currently £275,000.

INTESTATE When someone dies without leaving a valid will.

INDEMNIFY Whereby someone will guarantee to either carry out the terms of an agreement or to pay in the event of the first person defaulting.

INDENTURE A document written in duplicate on the same parchment or paper and divided into two by cutting through in a wavy line. The two parts can be fitted together to prove that they are genuine and are known as counterparts, formerly conveyancers where called indentures as were indentures for apprentices.

INDICTABLE OFFENCE An offence which can be tried by Jury in a Crown Court.

INCUMBRANCE Usually a mortgage on the property.

INJUNCTION A Writ prohibiting or commanding something not to be done or to be ceased from being done in the Civil courts.

INJUNCTION AND ORDER At which a party to an action is required to do or refrain from doing a particular thing.

JOINT & SEVERAL Where two or more parties are liable in the event of one defaulting the other is totally liable, and vice versa.

JOINT TENANTS Co-owners of property and the survivor automatically inherits in the event of the death of the first one.

LAND The Land incorporates all the buildings built upon it.

LEADING QUESTION A question which suggests the answer to be given or assumes things to be true which in fact are indisputable.

GLOSSARY

LEASEHOLD Held by a tenant with a lease.

LIEN The rights of one party to hold property until the performance of some obligation is completed, such as solicitors holding files and documents until their fees have been paid, similarly a garage when your car being fixed.

MEDIATION Help from an independent person to solve differences between say husband and wife.

MENS REA To commit a crime.

MERCHANTABLE QUALITY An assumption in the law that goods sold by a business will be fit for there purpose.

MISPRESENTATION A lie told to persuade someone to enter into a contract.

MITIGATION Putting facts to a judge after someone has been found guilty to justify a lower sentence.

NEGLIGENCE Lack of proper care to do a duty properly.

OVERRIDING INTEREST Right that other persons may have on the property.

PARCELS This is the usual description to describe pieces of land that has been divided up.

PER STIRPES Describes property divided equally between the offspring, therefore if the parent dies the child will get the share their parent would have got.

POACHING Taking game from someone else's land without permission.

PROBATE Authority to deal with a dead persons estate when some has died and left a will. The executors of the estate apply to the court for this authority.

PRIVATE TREATY Usually a sale made by Auction.

QUARTER DAYS When payment made every quarter should be paid. – 25th March Lady Day, 24th June – Midsummer day, 29th September – Michaelmas Day, 25th December – Christmas day.

QUIET ENJOYMENT Allowing a tenant to use land without interference. The landlord is expected allow the tenant to use the land without any interference unless the tenant's agreement allows it.

REAL As in Real Property relating to immovable property such as buildings or land.

REASONABLE FORCE Reasonable force is a complex issue where essentially use of some force may be necessary to defend you property or yourself. The force used must be in proportion to the threat.

REPUDITATION Means to refuse – to discharge an obligational debt.

RESIDENCE ORDERS An order, which a court issues when, is has decided where a child should live.

RESIDUARY LEGATEE What remains to be given out from an estate when all debts taxes and specific legacies have been paid.

RES IPSA LOQUITUR Proof is not needed because the facts speak for themselves.

RESCISSION Can mean order of the Court whereby the parties are put back into such a state as would have prevailed have the contract never existed, in effect the undoing of the contract. Made the order where the claim arising out of some factor such as fraud mistake or misrepresentation.

REASONABLE CHASTISMENT This is to do with children and again an area of law that is changing, may not cause a bruise or wound.

RESTRICTIVE COVENANT When referring to land it's a promise to do something, such as to use it for certain purposes.

RESTRICTIVE COVENANT – EMPLOYMENT There may be a term in the contract restricting you from taking up that trade within a certain period of time of within a certain area after you have left your previous employer. Must be reasonable.

RETENTION OF TITLE Another term for reservation of Title.

RIGHT OF WAY Legal right obliging the owner of land to allow authorised people to cross it.

ROOT OF TITLE Now an obsolete expression, which was used in unregistered conveyancing, whereby the seller had to prove that he had owned the title for the last 13 years and give documentary proof of this.

SEISEN/SEISED A legal terminology referring to the freehold.

GLOSSARY

SELLERS PACK Still in the process of being introduced by the government, whereby once the property is offered for sale, these items must be available for inspection by any potential purchaser. Still controversial.

SITTING TENANT Literally the tenant who as the right to stay in the property under a form of tenancy.

SINE DIE Indefinitely. If the case has been adjourned, Sine Die – no date has been set for it to be continued.

SLANDER Saying something untrue about a person or doing something such as making a gesture which damages their reputation.

SPECIFIC PERFORMANCE One of the remedies under a bridge of contract could be either specific performance or damages.

SQUATTER A person who occupies land illegally.

STATUE OF LIMITATIONS A statue which sets out the time limits in which a court action must be taken, three years for personal injury, usually six years for everything else.

STAKEHOLDER When a deposit is being held by a third party or in an account which does not immediately pass to the seller without the authority of the buyer.

STAMP DUTY The tax payable on deeds and documents, transfer of land.

STIPENDARY MAGISTRATE A magistrate who gets a salary.

SUBJECT TO CONTRACT An agreement, which is not binding until a contract, has been signed.

SUB JUDICE Describes something being dealt with by the court, which cannot be discussed outside the court.

SUMMARY OFFENCE An offence which only can be tried by a magistrate, most minor offences are summary offences.

TAX AVOIDANCE This is an attempt to re-arrange ones affairs so as to minimise liabilities within the narrow letter the full spirit of the law. This is legal.

TAX EVASION This involves a breach sometimes a dishonest and unlawful attempt to flout obligations.

TENURE Either Freehold or Leasehold, which is either Fee Simple Absolute in possession or for a term of years absolute.

TENANTS IN COMMON Property is owned in separate shares and each party can leave their share to whoever they wish.

TENANT FOR LIFE The person entitled to live at the property during their lifetime, after which it passes to another, usually under a will or trust.

TESTIMONIUM Formal word on the Attestation clause, that is where the parties sign.

TESTATOR A person who makes a will.

TESTACY – CO-HABITING COUPLES At the moment Co-habitant couples have no rights under Intestacy, the law is in a state of flux, and it may be that co-habits can make a claim if they were being maintained by the other party.

TIME OF THE ESSENCE Where a contract specifies the time for its completion, or something to be done towards it, then if time be of the essence of the contract, then non performance by either party of the act in question by the time so specified will entitle the opposite party to regard the contract as broken.

TITLE Legal evidence the owner owns the property.

TORT Doing something, which harms someone else – it may result in a claim for damages. It's an old French word.

TRESPASSING Going on land without the owner's permission.

TRUST A financial arrangement under which property is held by named people for someone else.

TRUSTESS FOR SALE When more than one person owns the estate, such as joint tenants and tenants in common, with joint tenant the survivor owns with tenants in common in receipt of more than one person.

UBERRIMAE FIDEI Of the utmost good faith, such as insurance contracts.

ULTRA VIRES Beyond ones powers. It is an organisation which does something invalid.

GLOSSARY

UNMARRIED PARENTS/ACQUIRING PARENTAL RESPONSIBILTY
The rules have changed recently, and I understand that an unmarried father may acquire parental responsibility by his name being put on the birth certificate, but normally he can obtain it by court order or the mother signing a parental responsibility form.

VACATING RECEIPT Formal expression for the receipts on a mortgage or legal charge.

VEXATIOUS LITIGANT A person who regularly brings Court cases which has little chance of succeeding.

VICARIOUS LIABILITY A situation where someone becomes responsible under the law for wrongs done by another. Usually employer for employee.

WILLS – CODICILS A codicil to a Will is merely an addition to a will, it has to be executed and exactly the same way as a will, that is in the presence of two independent witnesses.

WILLS – CO-HABITEES It is highly recommended that Cohabitees make wills to each other because the law at the moment does not automatically allow the cohabitee to inherit in the event of intestacy.

WITHOUT PREJUDICE A method of making offer or communicating with the other side without them being able to refer to these letters in any court action. The opposite of without prejudice is open correspondence.

INDEX

Abatement 114
Accidents 123
Accidents and sport 105
Accidents at works 102
Accidents in the street 102
Accidents in your rented home 101
Accidents involving children 103
Accidents involving visitors 101
Accidents of private property (private premises) 101
Accounting Records for Tax Purposes 132
Acknowledgement of testator's signature 111
Acknowledgement of witness's signature 111
Actus Reus 35
Administering poison 42
Adultery 85
Adverse possession 69
Advertisements for creditors 116
Advisory, conciliation and Arbitration Service ACAS 8
Aliens 54
Alternative dispute resolution 8
Alternative sources of compensation 100
Animus testandi (intention of making a will) 109
Appendix 137–140
Applying for the grant 117
Appointment of Guardians 112
Assault and Battery 41
Assets 128
Attestation clause 111–113

Barristers 5–9
Bars to divorce 86
Battery 55
Behaviour 85

Being bound by terms 92
Beneficiary as attesting witness 115
Bigamy 49
Blackmail 48
Boundaries and Fences 18 and 65
Breach of Statutory Duty 60
Breach of statutory restriction 76
Breach of Trust 51
Burden of Proof 38
Burglary 47
Business, You and Your 127–135
Buyers remedies 95
Buying a car from a dealer 12
Buying and selling your home 11–32
Buying at an auction 123
Buying privately 123

Capability 74
Capacity 108
Capacity 74
Capital Expenditure 133
Car alarms 64
Car theft 123
Car, You and Your
Careless driving 59
Careless driving offences 124
Categories of gift 114
Certificate of Insurance 131
Chancery Division of the High Court 2
Charging clause 113
Children 86
Children at school 104
Citizens Advice Bureau 7
Civil and criminal proceedings 100
Claiming compensation 105
Classification of Crimes 34
Codicils 108
Collection of assets 116

Common law 33
Commonhold 12
Community legal service 7
Competence of witnesses 111
Conciliation 98
Conditional fees 99
Conduct 74
Consanguinity and affinity 81–82
Consent orders 89
Consumer Law, You and Your Leisure
Consumer Protection 92
Continuity of employment 75
Contract and Formation 71
Contracts 14
Contributory negligence 103
Coroners courts 2
Corporate Liability 36
Corporations 54
County courts 2
Crime – definition of 33
Criminal damage 48
Criminal Injuries Compensation Board 50
Criminal law 33–50
Criminal Law, You and the Police
Criminal Liability 34
Criminal sanctions 93
Crown courts – appeals from magistrates courts 1

Dangerous Driving 40
Dangerous driving offences 124
Dangerous trees 68
Daughters in law 82
Dealings in shares of a Public Company 129
Death, You and Your
Debts 129
Decisions of directors 128
Decisions of shareholders 128
Defamation 61

Defences to a claim 102
Defences to a claim of negligence 100
Definition of a Tort 51
Desertion 85
Destruction 115
Disability Discrimination Act 93
Discrimination 93
Discriminations: Sex discrimination, equal pay and race discrimination 78
Dishonestly 38
Dismissal for health and safety activities 76
Dismissal – Procedure 76
Dispositions in the will 112
Distinction between keeper and owner of vehicle 120
Distribution 116
Divorce 84
Divorce law and procedure 86
Divorce reform 86
Donoghue and Stevenson (1932) 58
Drink drive offences 124
Driving under the influence of drink 50
Duration of periodical payments 88
Duty of care 58
Duty of care to passengers 59
Duty to Employees 78

Easement 7, 69
Emergency services 104
Employees 130
Employers liability insurance 102
Employment Law, You and Your Job
Employment tribunals, employment appeal tribunals 1
Enduring power of attorney – *see* Court of Protection 2
English Legal System, You and the Courts
European Law 93
Examples of Wills 112
Exchange of Contracts 15
Express Terms 71
Extended Warranty 94
Extension of trustee powers

Failure of gifts of property – ademption 114
False accounting 48
False imprisonment 55
Family Division of the High Court 2
Family, You and Your
Fences 66
Fixtures and Fittings 19
Forfeiture 114
Forgery 49
Formalities required by Statute 134
Freehold 12
Full and frank disclosure 121
Fundamental Characteristics 134
Funeral arrangements 112
Furniture Regulations 21
Future Dealings with Employees 131

Gas Regulations 21
Gender 82
General damages 105
Getting a refund 95
Gifts contained in a will
Gifts of land 114
Giving the Deceased the last word 139
Glossary 141–151
Goods and services 91
Goods must meet description 94
Grave hardship 86
Guarantees 94

Health and Safety 131
Health and Safety at Work 78, 79
Hedges and Ditches 66
Hedges Fence and Leyllandii 18
Highway authorities 102
Highways 102
HIPS 19
Home Information Pack (HIPS) 13

Home – Land Law, You and Your
House alarms 65
House of Lords 1, 3

Implied Terms 72, 92
In writing and signed by the testator 110
Inconsiderate driving 50
Indictable offences 34
Infanticide 40
Infants or Minors 54
Inheritance tax 117
Inheritance tax considerations 113
Insolvency 75
Insurance 132
Insurance certificate and driving licence 123
Insuring your car 120
Intellectual Property 132
Intent 38
Intention 85
Interference with goods 57
Involuntary manslaughter 40

Joint tenants 16
Judges – and the courts page 4
Judicial reviews 3
Judicial separation 87
Juries – *see* crown court 1
Justice court of the European Union 3

Land Law, You and Your Home
Landlords 20
Lawyers lack IT skills 137
Leased Covenants 21
Leasehold land 114
Leasehold/Freehold property 20
Legacies of bequest – gifts of personality 114
legal and Practical considerations when Starting a Business 130
Legal attempts to combat noise 63

INDEX

Legal Service Ombudsman 7
Leisure, You and Your
Licence and Consumer Credit Act 132
Licensed Conveyancers 6
Licensed to drive 119
Listed buildings 31
Listed Market 129
Litigation, You and Your
Lord Chancellor 4
Lump Sum Orders 88

Magistrates courts 1, 5
Mail order/E-commerce 95
Maintaining your car – offences 121
Malice 52
Malicious Wounding 42
Managing Tenants 26
Manslaughter page 39
Manufacturer's guarantee 95
Married Women 54
Maternity Leave 77
May a beneficiary be a witness? 111
Meaning of signature 110
Mediation 8, 87
Medical accidents 104
Mending fences 66
Mens Rea 37
Methods of Terminating a marriage 84
Minimum wage 72
Misconception – re Wills 107
Mistake 53
Motoring 125
Murder 39

Necessity 53
Negligence 37
Nervous shock 105
Noise as a form of pollution 63

Noise from children 65
Non Contractual arrangements 92
Nuisance 57
Nullity 84
Number plates 120

Oath 116
Obligation to the buyer 94
Obligations of the seller 93
Obligations to report an accident 123
Obtaining the grant 116
Occupiers liability 60, 101
Offences triable either way 34
Offer of Similar work 75
Omissions 36
Orders available at the court 87
Other Licences 132
Overhanging plants and trees 67

Parental leave 77
Parents liability 104
Partnership 127
Party Walls 67
Paying in advance by credit card 95
Payment of liabilities 116
Pensions 88
Periodical payments 88
Personal injury 99
Personal representatives 115
Persons of unsound mind 54
Planning 26, 27, 28, 29, 30, 31, 32
Polygamous marriages 83
Position of the Testator's signature 110
Potential exempt transfers 117
Powers and duties or personal representatives
Powers of appropriation 113
Powers of investment 113
Powers of maintenance and advancement 112
Powers to carry on a business 113

INDEX

Powers to purchase or retain a residence 113
Preparing the Will 109
Preservation of the peace 56
Preservation order 31
Private Limited Company 127
Privileged Wills 111
Privy council – Judicial Committee of 3
Probate glossary 118
Problems with children 101
Prohibited degrees 81
Property damage 105
Proposals for change 105
Protection, Court of 2
Protection from harassment 56
Proving the grounds 84
Public get direct access to the Bar 138
Public Limited Company 129
Public Nuisance 67
Publicity 129

Qualifying period 73
Queens Bench Division of the High Court 2
Queens Counsel 6

Random breath testing 124
Reasons for Dismissal 74
Receipts of the Trade less Income Expenditure 133
Receiver – *see* Court of Protection 2
Recent changes 137
Recent changes in the law 137
Recklessness 38
Redundancy 75
Registered Land 11
Rejecting the goods 95
Reliefs from tax 117
Remedies 76
Remedies for trespass to land 57
Remoteness of damage 54
Remuneration 72

Renewing your licence when aged 70 or over 120
Repeat offenders 125
Requirements of a valid marriage 81
Restrictions on marriage 81
Restrictive Covenants 17, 18
Revocation by dissolution or annulment of marriage
Revocation by marriage of remarriage
Revocation of wills 115
Right and duties on marriage 81
Robbery 46
Royal courts of Justice 2
Running a Business in Partnership 134

Safety legislation 103
Sale of Goods 93
Sale of Property 88
Sales 95
Satisfactory quality and fitness for purpose 93
Scope of employer's liability 103
Seat belts 122
Secured periodical payments 88
Self defence 53, 56
Seller must give title to the goods 94
Separation 85
Separation for five years 85
Setting up a partnership 134
Settlement of Property 88
Sexual offences 42, 43, 44
Short marriages 86
Shorthold Tenancy 24
Signing a contract 91
Signing of the Will 110
Single status 82
Sole Trader 127–133
Solicitors 5, 9
Solicitors Self Regulation 137
Some writing declaring an intention to revoke 115
Speeding offences 125

Splitting the Assets 89–90
Staff at risk from the public 103
Standard of Care – contributory negligence 60
Statutory Land Tax 12
Statutory Nuisance 67
Statutory requirements for a valid will 109
Step relations 82
Stolen cars 122
Stolen goods 47
Strength in numbers 139
Strict Liability 35
Strike Action 76
Summary offences 34
Surveyors 14

Taking a vehicle without consent, or 'joyriding' 123
Tax and national Insurance 131
Taxation 128
Taxation of Income and Income profits 133
Tenants in Common 17
Test of reasonableness 75
The Alternative Investment Market 130
The criminal law 82
The Decree 84
The European Convention of Human Rights 83
The 'MOT' test 122
The statutory background 87
The survivorship period 114
Theft 44, 45
Third party 120
time limits 100
Time off for dependants 77
Torts, law of
Trade associations and codes of practice 97
Trade Unions 54
Transfer of undertakings 75
Transsexual 83
Trespass 55

Trespass to land 56
Tribunals – employment etc. 1
Two years separation 85

Unfair or Wrongful Dismissal 73
Unwritten contracts 92

Vacant possession 17
Value Added Tax 132
Vicarious Liability 37, 55, 78
Void and Voidable Marriages 83
Volenti non-fit injuria 52
Voluntary manslaughter 39
Voluntary revocation 115

Welfare of the children 89
What is a partnership 134
What you can and can't do when driving your vehicle 120
Whistle blowing 77
Who may sign? 110
Wilfully 38
Will and Codicils 108
Working Time Regulations 72
Wounding with Intent 42
Written contracts 91
Wrongful dismissa 74

You and Your Business 127–135
You and Your Car – Motoring 119–125
You and Your Death – Will, Probate and Intestacy 107–118
You and Your Family – Matrimonial/Family Law 81–90
You and Your Leisure 91–93
You and Your Litigation 97–106
You and Your Job 71–79
You and Your Neighbours – Civil Law – The Law of Torts 51–62
You and Your Neighbours – The Neighbour Principle 63–69
Your car must be licensed too 120